SPECTRUM

3

A Communicative
Course in English

Diane Warshawsky
with Donald R. H. Byrd

Donald R. H. Byrd *Project Director*

Anna Veltfort *Art Director*

Longman

Library of Congress has cataloged the full edition of this title as follows:

Warshawsky, Diane.
    Spectrum 3, a communicative course in English / Diane Warshawsky
with Donald R. H. Byrd; Donald R. H. Byrd, project director; Anna
Veltfort, art director.
        p   cm.
Also published in a two-book split edition
ISBN 0-13-830068-2
    1. English language--Textbooks for foreign speakers.   I. Byrd,
Donald R. H. II. Title.
PE1128.W363   1994
428.3'4--dc20   93-26881
                                                                              CIP

        ISBN (3A)   0-13-830076-3   ISBN (3B)   0-13-830118-2

Project Manager: Nancy L. Leonhardt
Manager of Development Services: Louisa B. Hellegers
Editorial Consultant and Contributing Writer: Larry Anger
Contributing Writer: Susan Stempleski
Development Editor: Stephanie I. Karras
Audio Development Editor: D. Andrew Gitzy
Assistants to the Editors: Sylvia P. Bloch, Adam Hellegers, Amy Adrion

Managing Editor: Sylvia Moore
Production Editors and Compositors: Jan Sivertsen, Christine McLaughlin Mann
Technical Support and Assistance: Molly Pike Riccardi, David Riccardi, Ken Liao
Production Coordinator: Ray Keating
Production Assistant: Ellen Gratkowski, Wanda España
Cover Design: Roberto de Vicq
Interior Concept and Page-by-Page Design: Anna Veltfort

Audio Program Producer: Paul Ruben

©1994 by PRENTICE HALL REGENTS
A Pearson Education Company
Pearson Education
10 Bank Street
White Plains, NY 10606

Printed in the United States of America

20 19 18 17 16 15 14

ISBN 0-13-830068-2

INTRODUCTION

Welcome to the new edition of *Spectrum*! Spectrum 3 represents the third level of a six-level course designed for adolescent and adult learners of English. The student book, workbook, and audio program for each level provide practice in all four communication skills, with a special focus on listening and speaking. Levels 1 and 2 are appropriate for beginning students and "false" beginners. Levels 3 and 4 are intended for intermediate classes, and 5 and 6 for advanced learners of English. The first four levels are offered in split editions — 1A, 1B, 2A, 2B, 3A, 3B, 4A, and 4B.

Spectrum is a "communicative" course in English, based on the idea that communication is not merely an end-product of language study, but rather the very process through which a new language is acquired. *Spectrum* involves students in this process from the very beginning by providing them with useful, natural English along with opportunities to discuss topics of personal interest and to communicate their own thoughts, feelings, and ideas.

In *Spectrum*, comprehension is considered the starting point for communication. The student books thus emphasize the importance of comprehension, both as a useful skill and as a natural means of acquiring a language. Students begin each unit by listening to and reading conversations that provide rich input for language learning. Accompanying activities enhance comprehension and give students time to absorb new vocabulary and structures. Throughout the unit students encounter readings and dialogues containing structures and expressions not formally introduced until later units or levels. The goal is to provide students with a continuous stream of input that challenges their current knowledge of English, thereby allowing them to progress naturally to a higher level of competence.

Spectrum emphasizes interaction as another vital step in language acquisition. Interaction begins with simple communication tasks that motivate students to use the same structure a number of times as they exchange real information about themselves and other topics. This focused practice builds confidence and fluency and prepares students for more open-ended activities involving role playing, discussion, and problem solving. These activities give students control of the interaction and enable them to develop strategies for expressing themselves and negotiating meaning in an English-speaking environment.

The *Spectrum* syllabus is organized around functions and structures practiced in thematic lessons. Both functions and structures are carefully graded according to level of difficulty, and usefulness. Structures are presented in clear paradigms with informative usage notes. Thematic lessons provide interesting topics for interaction and a meaningful vehicle for introducing vocabulary.

This student book consists of fourteen units, each divided into one- and two-page lessons. Each unit begins with a preview page that outlines the functions/themes, language, and forms (grammar) in the unit. A preview activity prepares students to understand the cultural material in the conversations that begin each unit and gives them the opportunity to contribute their own background knowledge. The first lesson in each unit presents a series of realistic conversations, providing input for comprehension and language acquisition. New functions and structures are then practiced through interactive tasks in several thematic lessons. A one-page, fully illustrated comprehension lesson provides further input in the form of a dialogue and listening exercise both related to the storyline for the level. The next one-page lesson provides pronunciation practice and includes discussion or role-playing activities that draw on students' personal experience. The final lesson of the unit presents realistic documents such as historical texts and news articles for reading comprehension practice. There are review lessons after units 4, 7, 11, and 14. An accompanying workbook, audio cassette program, and teacher's edition are available.

For the preparation of the new edition, Prentice Hall Regents would like to thank the following long-time users of Spectrum, whose insights and suggestions have helped to shape the content and format of the new edition: Motofumi Aramaki, Sony Language Laboratory, Tokyo, Japan; Associacão Cultural Brasil-Estados Unidos (ACBEU), Salvador-Bahia, Brazil; AUA Language Center, Bangkok, Thailand, Thomas J. Kral and faculty; Pedro I. Cohen, Professor Emeritus of English, Linguistics, and Education, Universidad de Panamá; ELSI Taiwan Language Schools, Taipei, Taiwan, Kenneth Hou and faculty; James Hale, Sundai ELS, Tokyo, Japan; Impact, Santiago, Chile; Instituto Brasil-Estados Unidos (IBEU), Rio de Janeiro, Brazil; Instituto Brasil-Estados Unidos No Ceará (IBEU-CE), Fortaleza, Brazil; Instituto Chileno Norteamericano de Cultura, Santiago, Chile; Instituto Cultural Argentino Norteamericano (ICANA), Buenos Aires, Argentina; Christopher M. Knott, Chris English Masters Schools, Kyoto, Japan; The Language Training and Testing Center, Taipei, Taiwan, Anthony Y. T. Wu and faculty; Lutheran Language Institute, Tokyo, Japan; Network Cultura, Ensino e Livraria Ltda, São Paulo, Brazil; Seven Language and Culture, São Paulo, Brazil.

S C O P E A N D

S E Q U E N C E

LANGUAGE	FORMS	SKILLS
Do you know of any hotels around here? Yes, there's one on State Street. Did you have anything special in mind? Just someplace clean and inexpensive. Can you recommend a nice restaurant in this neighborhood? Which one is the nicest? The Harvest is the nicest, but it's also the most expensive. What's the best way to get to The Harvest? You can either walk or take a bus. It's about a thirty-minute walk or fifteen minutes by bus. So, it's faster by bus. Could you please tell me how to get to Toby's "Good Eats"? When you get to Yorkville, turn left. Stay on Bellair until you get to Bloor Street. You can't miss it.	Indefinite compounds with adjectives The superlative of adjectives Comparatives vs. superlatives Future time clauses with the simple present tense: *when, just before, just after, as soon as,* and *until*	Listen to advice Listen for recommendations Listen for directions Listen to the intonation of statements and questions Read a magazine article Write a response to a letter (workbook)
I have to be at a meeting at noon. I'm supposed to pick up the kids at 5:00. I'd better go. If my son calls, tell him to be ready at six. Could you explain them to me? Would you do me a favor? Would you please give this note to Mary for me? Would you explain this to me? O.K. Oh, I'll call her for you. I'll introduce you to him. Could you show me how to work the VCR? I'm not sure how to record. Sure. I'd be glad to. May I speak to Ms. Clark, please? May I tell her who's calling? Would you have her call me when she gets back?	*Have to* and *be supposed to* *Had better* Two-word verbs *Could* *Would* Indirect objects with *to* and *for* Direct and indirect objects Question words with infinitives	Listen to instructions Listen to a request Listen to a phone message Listen to vowel and consonant reduction and blending with the pronouns *him* and *her* Read a newspaper article Write a letter to a friend (workbook)
Do you ever get any exercise? I ought to exercise more, but I can never seem to find the time. I've always enjoyed swimming. I hate getting up early on weekends. Has he lost (a lot of) weight? Yeah. Twenty pounds. That's great! How tall is he? Five foot ten. I'm going biking with Bill and a friend of ours on Saturday. How about joining us? Do you know where I can rent a bike? She's a lot like me. She's very different from me. Did you use to get along when you were younger? Not too well.	Infinitives vs. gerunds Possessive pronouns and possessives of names The past with *used to*	Listen for preferences Listen to a description of someone Listen to the different pronunciations of the possessive *s* Read a magazine article Write a response to a letter (workbook)
Review	Review	Review
I hope I didn't wake you up. I was just watching TV. Are you doing anything on Saturday? How about coming over (for dinner) on Saturday? What time do you want us to come? I hope (that) you can make it. I don't think (that) I'm busy. But let me check my calendar. We have theater tickets for Saturday, don't we? He'd like us to come over later. What does he do again? He's the one who just got married.	The past continuous *Hope and think* Tag questions Infinitives after object pronouns	Listen for what people were doing Listen for information about people's plans Listen to the intonation of statements and questions Read an advice column Write a letter (workbook)
I was bored most of the time. The restaurants were a little disappointing. You really ought to go to Brazil. You won't be disappointed. It's in the southern part of the country. It's about 600 miles southwest of Rio de Janeiro. Would anyone care for coffee? Here are some sandwiches. Help yourselves. Who's the woman standing behind Jack? She's someone (who, that) we met at the park.	Present participles and past participles used as adjectives *Ought to* Relative clauses	Listen for opinions Listen to people accept and decline food Listen for descriptions of people Listen to the pronunciation of adjectives ending -ing Read encyclopedia entries Write a travel advertisement (workbook)

LANGUAGE	FORMS	SKILLS
I'm calling about the apartment you advertised. Could you tell me more about it? The living room's eighteen by twenty-three feet. Does it say how much it is? It's $725 a month. No, it doesn't. Could you tell me what floor it's on? It's on the second floor. Could you tell me which bus goes to the Fine Arts Museum? Do you know how often the Number 1 bus runs during rush hour? Every five minutes or so. I have no idea. Do you know where Oak Street is? It's off Washington, near the park. I'd rather live in an older building. I'd rather not live in a modern building.	Embedded questions Prepositions *I'd rather* and *I'd rather not*	Listen for information about the size of an apartment Listen for information about a bus schedule Listen for preferences Listen to the intonation of statements and questions Read a magazine article Write a classified ad (workbook)
Do you have any plans for the weekend? It depends on the weather. If it's nice, I'll go to the beach. If it isn't, I'll stay home and catch up on some reading. If you need a ride to the airport, I'll be happy to drive you. I'm thinking of flying, but it depends on how much it costs. Could you speak a little louder? How come? I couldn't get a later flight. I'd like some information about morning flights from Bangkok to Taipei.	Conditional sentences Embedded questions The comparative of adverbs *Couldn't*	Listen to offers Listen to an airline reservation Listen to the pronunciation of conditional sentences Read a magazine article Write about plans (workbook)
Review	Review	Review
This must be a great place to eat! Do you know what you're going to order? I can't make up my mind. I'm going to get the cherry cheesecake. Could I have another cup of coffee, please? I'll get it for you right away. Could we have some more water, please? Of course. How's your lobster? It tastes kind of funny. Mmm. Delicious. It smells awful. He looks familiar, but I'm not sure who he is. Do you mind if I open the window? No, not at all. I'd rather you didn't.	*Must* *Another, some/any more*, and *something/anything else* with count and mass nouns Sense verbs	Listen for preferences Listen for opinions Listen to vowel and consonant reduction and blending in *could you, would you,* and *why don't you* Read a restaurant guide Write a thank-you note (workbook)
I've been sneezing all day. You must be getting a cold. What did I do with my glasses? They may be in your coat pocket. What are you doing this weekend? I might play tennis. Do we have any cough medicine? There's only a little left. There's not much left. We must not have any more then. Is there anything you need? Could you pick up a roll of paper towels? Could you tell me where the carrots are? They're behind the lettuce. It's on the top shelf, next to the spaghetti. They're in the refrigerator, on the bottom shelf. I'm sorry I'm late. I got caught in traffic. I just got here myself. Oh, that's O.K.	*Must* *May* and *might* Count and mass nouns Prepositions	Listen for location Listen to weekend plans Listen to the pronunciation of compound nouns Read an advice column Write a business memo (workbook)
I haven't seen you in so long! How have you been? You haven't changed a bit! I didn't recognize you at first. You've really changed! Do you still keep in touch with anyone from school? I still get together with Rosa from time to time. No, I've really lost touch with everyone. Have you seen any good movies recently? No, not in a long time. Neither have I. Yes, I've seen a couple of good ones. How long have you been living in Toronto? I've been living here since last fall. Why don't we go get coffee somewhere? Good idea. Let's go to the coffee shop on the corner. I'd like to, but I've got to get going.	Review: The present perfect Short negative responses The present perfect continuous	Listen to people greet each other after a long time Listen for information about people's past activities Listen to consonant reduction and blending in *gotten, written,* and *eaten* Read a magazine article Write a short letter to an old friend (workbook)
Review	Review	Review

PREVIEW

FUNCTIONS/THEMES	LANGUAGE	FORMS
Introduce someone	Have you met Marie? Yes, I have. Have you two met each other? No, I don't believe we have.	The present perfect: yes-no questions and short answers
Say how you know someone	We used to work together. We both teach at Kennedy High School. We're from the same hometown.	Formulaic use of *used to*
Say hello informally	How are you doing, Ted? Hi, Julia. Nice to see you.	
Talk about places you've been	Have you ever been to San Francisco? Yes, I've been there many times.	Past participles of some irregular verbs
Talk about things you've done	Have you ever gone snorkeling? No, I haven't. Have you? Yes, I have.	
Offer help Accept or decline help	Here, let me help you with that. Oh, thanks. That's very nice of you. That's O.K. I can manage.	Offers with *let*
Strike up a conversation	I hear you got a new job. Yes, I just started this week. I see you're reading *Time* magazine. I just got it this morning.	*Just* for the recent past
End a conversation	Enjoy yourself! It's been nice talking to you. I've enjoyed talking to you.	

Preview the conversations.

Where are the people in the pictures? Why are they there? Which people know each other? Which people don't know each other? What is happening in the second picture?

Imagine you are one of the people in the pictures. With two other classmates, act out the conversation.

1. Taking off

 United Airlines Flight 856 is flying from Seattle, Washington, to Chicago, Illinois.

A

Laura Enders Jim Blake! What a surprise!

Jim Blake I don't believe it. What are you doing here in Seattle?

Laura Oh, I just spent a few days with my parents. Now I'm on my way back to Chicago.

Jim Gee, it's been a long time.

Laura It sure has. Say, I hear you started your own computer business.

Jim How did you know?

Laura My mother. She keeps track of all my old friends.

B

Monica Blake (*Coughs*)

Jim Oh, I'm sorry. Have you two met each other?

Laura No, I don't believe we have.

Jim Laura, this is my wife, Monica. Monica, I'd like you to meet Laura Enders. Laura and I went to high school together.

Monica It's nice to meet you, Laura.

Laura Nice to meet you, too.

Announcer (*Over loudspeaker*) United Airlines Flight 856 to Chicago is now boarding at Gate 9.

Laura Oh, that's my flight. I have to go.

Monica We've got a plane to catch, too.

Laura Where are you off to?

Monica We're taking a week off and going to Hawaii.

Laura Oh, really? Have you been there before?

Monica Yes, a few times.

Laura Well, enjoy yourselves.

Monica Thanks, we will.

Laura Great seeing you, Jim. Nice meeting you, Monica.

Jim Same here.

Monica and Jim Bye.

C

Doug Lee I see you're reading the new Stephen King novel. How do you like it?

Laura I can't put it down. Have you read it?

Doug Yes. As a matter of fact, I just finished it. The ending's great.

Laura Don't tell me! I'm almost done.

Doug Are you from Chicago?

Laura Well, I'm originally from Seattle, but I live in Chicago now.

Doug How do you like it?

Laura Very much. Have you ever been to Chicago before?

Doug No, I haven't. This is my first trip. I have a job interview there. By the way, my name's Doug Lee.

Laura I'm Laura Enders.

D

Flight attendant Here, let me help you get that down.

Laura Oh, thanks. That's very kind of you.

Doug Well, it's been nice talking to you, Laura.

Laura I've enjoyed talking to you, too, Doug. Good luck on your interview.

Doug Thanks. I really want this job.

Figure it out

1. Listen to the conversations and choose the correct answers.

1. Jim and Laura
   a. have known each other a long time.
   b. haven't known each other a long time.

2. Doug and Laura
   a. have known each other a long time.
   b. haven't known each other for very long.

2. Read the sentences. Listen to the conversations again and say *True* or *False*.

1. Laura lives in Seattle.   *False.*
2. Jim and Laura are from the same hometown.
3. Laura and Monica have met before.
4. Doug has read the new Stephen King novel.
5. Doug has a job in Chicago.

3. Do the sentences in each pair have the same meaning or different meanings? Say *Same* or *Different*.

1. Where are you off to?
   Where are you going?   *Same.*

2. I just finished it.
   I finished it a long time ago.

3. What are you doing here in Seattle?
   Why are you here in Seattle?

4. We're taking a few days off.
   We're not going to work for a few days.

5. Have you been to Chicago before?
   Are you from Chicago?

6. Have fun!
   Enjoy yourselves!

2. Have you two met each other?

► A group of people are at the airport, waiting for a tour to depart. Listen to the conversation and complete the chart.

	Ted	Marie	Julia	John
Who used to work together?	√	√		
Who teaches at Kennedy High School?				
Who is from the same hometown?				
Who went to college together?				

► **Say how the people know each other.**
Ted and Marie used to work together.

► **Listen to the conversation.**
► **In groups of four, practice the conversation.**

John Hi, Julia. Have you met Ted?
Julia Yes, I have. We both teach at Kennedy High School. How are you doing, Ted?
Ted Hi, Julia. Nice to see you.
John Julia, have you met Marie?
Julia No, I haven't.
John This is Marie Jones. Marie has her own advertising agency. Marie, I'd like you to meet Julia Rivera. Julia's a teacher. She and I are from the same hometown.
Marie Nice to meet you, Julia.

► **Interview three classmates and take notes. Ask the questions below or your own questions.**

1. Where are you from originally?
2. Where do you work?/Where do you live?
3. How long have you been at this school?

► **Now listen to the two possible conversations.**
► **Introduce the classmates you interviewed above.**

A Have you two met each other?

B No, I don't believe we have.

A Alex, this is Amy Tang. Amy's from Taiwan. Amy, I'd like you to meet Alex Garcia. Alex is from California.

B Nice to meet you, Amy.

C Nice to meet you, too.

B Yes, we have. We were in the same class last term.

4 ▶ **Listen to the two possible conversations.**
▶ **Work with a partner. Find out if your partner has been to these or other cities.**

San Francisco   Rio de Janeiro   Bangkok

A Have you ever been to San Francisco?

B Yes, I've been there many times. Have you?   **B** No, I never have. Have you?

A Yes, I was just there last week.   **A** No, I haven't.

I've been there	once. twice. a few times. many times.

5 ▶ **Study the frames: The present perfect**

Yes-no questions		
Have	I you we they	**met** Julia? **been** to San Francisco?
Has	he she	

Short answers		
Yes,	you I we they	**have**.
No,		**haven't**.
Yes,	he	**has**.
No,	she	**hasn't**.

Past participles of some irregular verbs

Base form	Simple past	Past participle
be (am, is, are)	was, were	**been**
do	did	**done**
eat	ate	**eaten**
go	went	**gone**
have	had	**had**
hear	heard	**heard**
leave	left	**left**
meet	met	**met**
read [rid]	read [rɛd]	**read** [rɛd]
ride	rode	**ridden**
see	saw	**seen**
take	took	**taken**

6 ▶ **Complete the conversation. Use the present perfect of the verbs in parentheses or short answers.**
▶ **Listen to check your work.**

Marie _Have you taken_ (take) a tour before?

Julia Yes, _I have_ . I went to Europe with a group last year. _____ (be) to Europe?

Marie Yes, _____ , but only to London on business. I'm really excited about this trip.

Julia Me too. _____ (see) all the brochures?

Marie Yes. I can't wait to see all those places. By the way, _____ (meet) Scott, our tour guide?

Julia No, _____ . I think he's Australian. What do you know about him?

Marie Not much. _____ (hear) this is his second or third tour, and everybody seems to like him. Come on and I'll introduce you.

Julia Great.

7 ▶ **In small groups, make a list of the different countries your classmates have been to. Then, under the name of each country, write the names of the cities your classmates have visited.**

3. Have you ever gone snorkeling?

1 ▶ Find out which tour the group is going on. Listen to the radio commercial and circle *Pacific Tour A* or *Pacific Tour B*.

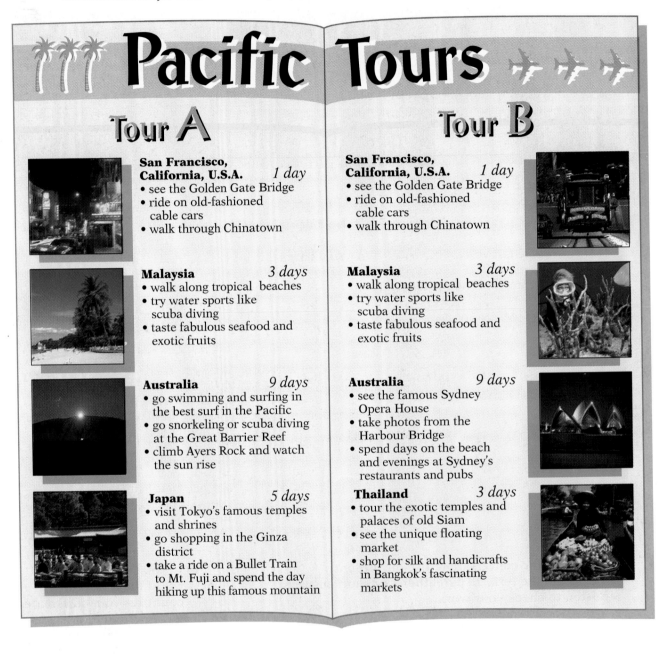

Pacific Tours

Tour A

San Francisco, California, U.S.A.   *1 day*
- see the Golden Gate Bridge
- ride on old-fashioned cable cars
- walk through Chinatown

Malaysia   *3 days*
- walk along tropical beaches
- try water sports like scuba diving
- taste fabulous seafood and exotic fruits

Australia   *9 days*
- go swimming and surfing in the best surf in the Pacific
- go snorkeling or scuba diving at the Great Barrier Reef
- climb Ayers Rock and watch the sun rise

Japan   *5 days*
- visit Tokyo's famous temples and shrines
- go shopping in the Ginza district
- take a ride on a Bullet Train to Mt. Fuji and spend the day hiking up this famous mountain

Tour B

San Francisco, California, U.S.A.   *1 day*
- see the Golden Gate Bridge
- ride on old-fashioned cable cars
- walk through Chinatown

Malaysia   *3 days*
- walk along tropical beaches
- try water sports like scuba diving
- taste fabulous seafood and exotic fruits

Australia   *9 days*
- see the famous Sydney Opera House
- take photos from the Harbour Bridge
- spend days on the beach and evenings at Sydney's restaurants and pubs

Thailand   *3 days*
- tour the exotic temples and palaces of old Siam
- see the unique floating market
- shop for silk and handicrafts in Bangkok's fascinating markets

2 ▶ Work with a partner. Find out if your partner has done any of the things described in the two tours.

A *Have you ever gone snorkeling?*
B *No, I haven't. Have you?*
A *. . .*

3 ▶ Plan a trip. Work in small groups. Imagine you are going to take one of the tours above. Decide which tour to take. Tell the class which tour you chose and why.

4. Let me help you with that.

OFFER HELP • ACCEPT OR DECLINE HELP • OFFERS WITH *LET*

1
▶ Complete each exchange with an offer from the box.
▶ Listen to check your work.

Let me help you . . .

a. get those down.
b. put that up.
c. carry something.
d. move that.

2
▶ Listen to the conversations. Does the person accept or decline the offer?

	Accept	Decline
1.	√	
2.		
3.		
4.		

3
▶ Listen to the two possible conversations.
▶ Practice the conversations with a partner.

A Here, let me help you with that.

B Oh, thanks. That's very kind of you.   **B** That's all right. I can manage.

Other ways to say it

Would you like some help with . . . ?
Can I help you with that?

Some ways to accept help	Some ways to decline help
Thanks. That's very kind of you.	I'm all set. But thanks anyway.
I appreciate it.	That's all right. I can manage.
That's really nice of you.	That's O.K. I've got it.

4
▶ Work with a partner. Act out the conversation.
Student A: Imagine you are the person in the picture.
Student B: Offer to help.

5. I see you're reading *Time* magazine.

▶ **These people are traveling on trains, planes, and buses. Listen to the four conversations. Write the number of the conversation next to the correct picture.**

▶ **Listen to the conversation and practice it with a partner.**
▶ **Strike up a conversation and try to keep it going.**

A I hear you've got a new job.
B Yes, I just started.

Some ways to strike up a conversation	Some ways to respond
With anyone:	
I see you're wearing a T-shirt from Temple University.	Yes, I go to school there.
I see you're reading *Time* magazine.	Yes, I just picked it up.
That's an interesting necklace.	Thanks. It's from Mexico.
With someone you know:	
I hear you got a new job.	Yes, I just started.
I hear you went to Brazil.	Yes, I just got back.

3 ► **Two people are on a flight from Toronto to New York. Play the roles below.**

Student A: You live in New York. You arrange concert tours for musicians. You've been on a business trip.

1. Start a conversation with the person next to you. The person is reading *The Wall Street Journal*.
2. Find out where the person is from.
3. Find out what kind of work the person does.
4. Find out if the person has been to New York before.
5. Continue the conversation, answer the other person's question, and tell about yourself.

Student B: You're on a business trip to the U.S. The person next to you starts a conversation.

1. You live in Montreal.
2. You work for a Canadian company that makes stereo equipment.
3. You spent a year in Toronto studying sound engineering.
4. Find out if the person next to you has ever been to Montreal.
5. Continue the conversation, answer the other person's questions, and tell about yourself.

4 ► **Work with a partner. Listen to these two conversations. Decide which conversation ends and which one continues.**

1. **A** It's been nice talking to you.
   B I've enjoyed talking to you, too.
   A Enjoy your stay in New York.
   B Thanks, I will.

2. **B** Have you ever been to Montreal?
   A No, but I'd like to go there. My friends say the night life is great there.
   B It is! We have terrific nightclubs and restaurants.
   A Really?

5 ► **Imagine that you are traveling on an airplane. Strike up a conversation with a partner. Find out where your partner is from and where he or she is going. Tell a little about yourself. Then end the conversation.**

Some ways to end a conversation	Other ways to say it
I've enjoyed talking to you. It's been nice talking to you. Enjoy your trip (your stay)! Enjoy yourself (yourselves)!	Have fun! Have a good time!

6. How have you been?

Laura Enders runs into a friend outside her health club.

1

Roger	Laura!
Laura	Oh, hi, Roger.
Roger	How have you been?
Laura	Fine.
Roger	I hear you went back to Seattle for a few days.
Laura	Yes, I just got back yesterday.
Roger	Did you have a nice visit?
Laura	Really nice. It was good being back home and just relaxing. My brother Mark was there, too. You've met Mark, haven't you?
Roger	Sure. I met him when he was here in Chicago last year. What's he up to these days? Still playing the guitar?
Laura	Yes. As a matter of fact, he just started his own band. How's everything with you and Carol?
Roger	Great.
Laura	How are the kids?
Roger	They're both fine.
Laura	Gee, I haven't seen them in so long. They must be really big.
Roger	Well, why don't you come over sometime? Carol and the kids would love to see you.
Laura	I'll do that. I'll give Carol a call during the week.

2. Figure it out

Say *True, False,* or *It doesn't say.*

1. Laura knows Roger and his family.
2. Laura just visited Seattle.
3. Roger knows Mark.
4. Laura plays the guitar.
5. Laura just called Roger's wife.

3. Listen in

Read the statement below. Then listen to another conversation taking place nearby. Choose *a, b,* or *c*.

These people are talking mainly about
a. a play.
b. a movie.
c. an actor.

7. Your turn

Work in groups. Discuss places you've visited and things you've done. Read the sample conversation before you begin.

A Have you ever been to Mexico City?
B Yes. I went with some friends last summer.
A How did you like it?
B It was beautiful. Have you ever been there?
A No, but I'd like to go someday.

Mexico City is the largest city in the world.

Elephants are found in the wild in parts of Africa and Asia. Most people see them in zoos, such as this one in San Diego, California.

Thousands of fans attend rock concerts. Although many new groups are popular, some older bands and musicians, such as Eric Clapton, still attract large crowds.

Euro Disney is one of the four internationally popular Disney amusement parks around the world. There is also a Disney park in Japan, as well as two in the U.S.—one in California and one in Florida.

Windsurfing is a sport that combines the skills of surfing and sailing. Here, windsurfers enjoy the waters off the coast of Brazil.

How to say it

Practice the past participles and phrases. Then practice the exchanges. Ask questions using the phrases.

been [bɪn] . . . been to Euro Disney?
seen [sin] . . . seen an elephant?
gone [gɔn] . . . gone to a soccer game?

had [hæd] . . . had a desire to travel?
eaten [ítn] . . . eaten at a McDonald's?
read [rɛd] . . . read anything by Stephen King?

A Have you ever been to Euro Disney?
B Yes, I have.

A Have you ever seen an elephant?
B No, I haven't.

8.

GETAWAY EMPLOYEE OF THE MONTH

Getaway **magazine spoke with Josef Schmidt, our travel agent in Hamburg, Germany, about his many travels.**

GETAWAY: We hear you've traveled to nearly forty different countries. Tell us, what has been your favorite place to visit?

SCHMIDT: Oh, I'd have to say Prague. I've always loved exploring old cities, and Prague is one of the most beautiful in terms of architecture. There are fantastic castles and museums that are relatively unknown to most tourists.

GETAWAY: Is there any one place that is particularly memorable for you?

SCHMIDT: That would probably be northern Mali, in the Sahara Desert. I spent New Year's Eve there once, and I remember watching the sun set over the sand dunes. When the stars came out, they were incredibly bright. I felt very far from home but very close to nature. It was completely different from any place I've ever been.

GETAWAY: What's your next destination?

SCHMIDT: I'm thinking about Australia. I've never been there. I'd love to go to the Great Barrier Reef and do some diving. And I've always wanted to see the Sydney Opera House.

GETAWAY: Of course they speak English in Australia, but how do you deal with all the different languages in other places you visit?

SCHMIDT: Well, I learned German at home and English at school. I find that I can pick up many phrases and expressions as I travel. If I know I'll be staying in one country for a while, I try to get a book or tape of the language to study. I'm fluent in Italian now, but I've also picked up quite a bit of Spanish, French, and Russian along the way.

GETAWAY: Has there been any place where you've had a lot of trouble with the language?

SCHMIDT: I was in China last year and yes, I had some difficulty there. Chinese is so very different from the languages I've studied, and of course the writing system is completely different. I had to use a lot of gestures and sign language.

GETAWAY: Is it hard to adjust to the different customs and people you meet?

SCHMIDT: I go with an open mind. I like to try new things. The first thing I always do when I get to a new place is buy a map. Then I'm ready to start on my new adventure.

The Old City of Prague

1. Scan the article for answers to these questions.

1. How many countries has Josef Schmidt been to?
2. How many languages does he speak?

2. Discuss these questions in a group.

1. On which continent do you think Josef Schmidt has done most of his traveling?
2. How does he prepare for his travels? Do you think his preparations are useful?
3. How do you adjust to different languages and customs when you travel or meet foreign tourists?

PREVIEW

FUNCTIONS/THEMES	LANGUAGE	FORMS
Talk about jobs and places you've lived	How long have you lived in Clinton? For three years. How long have you worked as a hairstylist? Since high school.	The present perfect information questions and statements with *for* and *since* The present perfect vs. the simple past tense
Talk about your fantasies	I've always wanted to go hiking in the Himalayas.	The present perfect
Talk about your family	Do you have any brothers and sisters? I have four older brothers and two older sisters. I'm the youngest. Two of them live in California. The others live in Chicago.	Partitives, *the other one,* and *the others*

Preview the conversations.

Clinton Students Start Summer Jobs

CLINTON, July 1—Summer has started, but Clinton college students and recent high school graduates are spending their vacations working. Ann Rutgers, the manager of Templine, a temporary employment agency, notes that many of the students are working to help pay for their college tuition and the others want to work for the experience.

"I've done office work for the last two summers," said Donna Lucas. "It's a little boring, but it's a change from schoolwork."

Jim Wright couldn't find a job in the construction business, so he took this job as a waiter in a local restaurant. "I've never worked as a waiter before," Jim said, "so I'm not sure if I'm going to like it or not. Ask me again at the end of the summer."

May Huang is working as a volunteer at a summer camp. "I've always wanted to work with kids," May told the reporter. "I'm getting great experience."

Read the article and discuss the questions.
1. Do high school and college students in your country have jobs during vacations?
2. If so, what kind of jobs do they have?
3. Have you ever had a temporary job?
4. If so, tell a partner what you did and if you enjoyed it.

9. How long have you been a waitress?

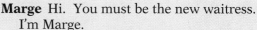 Tina Marco is starting a summer job as a waitress at Frank's Restaurant.

A

Marge Hi. You must be the new waitress. I'm Marge.
Tina Hi, Marge. I'm Tina.
Marge Do you go to Clinton High, Tina?
Tina I'm starting this fall. I'll be a senior. I've only lived here since the beginning of June.
Marge Really? Where did you live before?
Tina Texas.
Marge Well, welcome to Clinton.
Tina Thanks.

B

Tina How long have you lived in Clinton?
Marge Me? My whole life. You know Frank, the owner? We've known each other for thirty-five years . . . since kindergarten.
Tina No kidding! Have you ever wanted to live somewhere else?
Marge When I was younger I wanted to move to Hollywood and be an actress. But here I am . . . still in Clinton and still a waitress.
Tina Oh, that's funny. I've always wanted to be an actress, too. How long have you been a waitress?
Marge For twenty years now.
Tina That's a long time.
Marge You're telling me. I've always wanted to try a different kind of work. I make pretty good money as a waitress, though, so I just never have.
Tina Where else have you worked, or have you always worked here?
Marge Oh, no. Frank's only had this place since last year. Before that, I worked at the Clinton Hotel.

C

Joe Hi, Tina. How's it going?

Tina Oh, Joe, hi!

Marge Who's that good-looking guy? Your boyfriend?

Tina No. That's my brother Joe.

Marge Is he older or younger than you?

Tina He's a year older. I'm the youngest in the family.

Marge Oh, so you have other brothers and sisters . . .

Tina Yes, I have two other older brothers besides Joe and one older sister. But none of them live at home anymore.

Marge Oh, are they all married?

Tina Only my oldest brother, Tony. The others are away at college.

Marge I've always wanted to have brothers and sisters.

Tina You don't have any?

Marge No, I'm an only child.

Figure it out

1. Listen to the conversations. Then choose the correct sentence.

1. Tina is a student and has a temporary job as a waitress.
2. Tina has been a waitress for a long time.

2. Listen again. Are the statements about *Marge*, *Tina*, or *Both* of them?

1. She has three older brothers.   *Tina*.
2. She has lived in Clinton all her life.
3. She works for Frank.
4. She is in high school.
5. She is an only child.
6. She lived in Texas before.

3. Match.

1. Marge and Frank have known each other ———————
2. Marge has lived in Clinton
3. Tina has lived in Clinton
4. Frank has owned his restaurant

   a. since last year.
   b. for thirty-five years.
   c. her whole life.
   d. since the beginning of June.

10. How long have you lived in Clinton?

1 ► **Listen and select the employment application of the person being interviewed.**

Name John Hill
Position Desired Store Manager

Current Position Manager
Puppy Love Pet Shop, Clinton

1 year— since he moved here

Previous Experience Salesclerk
Best Pets, Toronto

Education Seneca College
Toronto

Name Paul Jacobs
Position Desired Hair Stylist

Current Position Hair Stylist
New Wave Beauty Salon
Clinton

3 years

Previous Experience Hair Stylist
Kindest Cuts
Washington, D.C.

Education Martin Luther King
High School
Washington, D.C.

2 ► **Listen to the conversation and practice it with a partner.**
► **Act out a similar conversation with information from the other application in exercise 1.**

A How long have you lived in Clinton?
B For three years.
A Where did you live before?
B In Washington, D.C.
A Where are you working now?
B At New Wave Beauty Salon.
A How long have you worked there?
B Since I moved to Clinton. Before that, I worked at Kindest Cuts in Washington.

3 ► **Study the frames: The present perfect**

Information questions				
	have	you they	**worked**	at New Wave?
How long			**lived**	in Clinton?
	has	he she	**wanted**	to move?

Statements with *for* and *since*					
I We They	**'ve**	**worked**	at New Wave		
		lived	in Clinton	for two years.	
He She	**'s**	**wanted**	to move	since high school.	

The past participle of regular verbs is the same as the simple past tense form.

have	've
has	's
he's	= he is *or* he has
she's	= she is *or* she has

4 ▶ **Complete the conversation with information questions and *for* or *since*.**
  ▶ **Listen to check your work.**

Ray You did a great job on that last customer,
  Paul. _how long_ (be) a hairstylist?
Paul _since_ I finished high school. I worked at New
  Wave before, but I've wanted to work here for
  a long time.
Ray Well, I hope you stay here.
Paul _How long_ (had) this business?
Ray _since_ we moved here from Washington, D.C.,
  about six years ago. Lois and I lived in
  Washington _for_ a few years before we came
  to Clinton.
Paul Oh, yeah? I lived in Washington before, too. I
  worked at Kindest Cuts.
Ray I know that place. Did you work with Jean
  Martin?
Paul Sure I did. _how long_ (know) Jean?
Ray _since_ we were kids. We still keep in touch.

5 ▶ **Study the frame: The present perfect vs. the simple past tense**

The present perfect: something that began in the past and continues into the present	The simple past tense: something completed in the past
Paul has been a hairstylist since he finished high school. (He is a hairstylist now.)	He worked at New Wave before. (He doesn't work there anymore.)
Ray has lived in Clinton for six years. (He still lives in Clinton.)	He lived in Washington, D.C., for a few years. (He doesn't live in Washington anymore.)

6 ▶ **Listen to Ray talk about himself. Then put the events in order.**

_4_ moved to Clinton
_6_ got jobs in Hollywood
_3_ got married to Lois
_5_ moved to California

_8_ moved back to Washington, D.C.
_9_ got the salon in Clinton
_1_ graduated from high school
_7_ got into the hairstyling business

7 ▶ **Tell a classmate about Ray.**

Ray's been in the hairstyling business for thirty years.
He got his first job right after high school.

8 ▶ **Interview two classmates. Find out where
  they've lived and what they've done.**

Other ways to say it	
for . . .	since . . .
ten years	1992
a long time	I left school

11. I've always wanted to be a rock star.

1

▶ **Work with a partner. Look at the pictures and guess who has always wanted to**

____ be a rock star.
____ go hiking in the Himalayas.
____ work in the construction business.
____ write TV soap operas.

▶ **Listen and match the people with their fantasies.**

1 Ellen Hanson
Bookkeeper
London, England

2 Luigi Contini
Systems Analyst
Rome, Italy

3 Carol Valentine
Graphic Artist
Atlanta, Georgia

4 Peter Yang
College Teacher
Taipei, Taiwan

2

▶ **Listen to the conversations and practice them with a partner.**

1. A I've always wanted to go hiking in the Himalayas.
   B Really? You know, I've always wanted to travel, too.

2. A I've always wanted to write TV soap operas.
   B That's funny. I've always wanted to be in show business, too.

3

▶ **Work with a partner. Look at the pictures below and act out conversations like the ones in exercise 2.**

4

▶ **Talk to two classmates. Find out where they have always wanted to go or what they have always wanted to do. Report to the class.**

Luisa has always wanted to take flying lessons.
Ali has always wanted to go to Italy.

12. Do you have any brothers and sisters?

TALK ABOUT YOUR FAMILY • PARTITIVES, *THE OTHER ONE, AND THE OTHERS*

1
► Listen and label the picture with the names.

a. Rose
b. Carl
c. Sue
d. Frank
e. Pat (the speaker)

2
► Listen to the two possible conversations and practice them with a partner.
► Act out a similar conversation with your partner. Use your own information.

A Do you have any brothers and sisters?

B I have four older brothers and two older sisters. I'm the youngest in the family.

B No, I'm an only child.

I'm . . .   the middle child   the oldest   the youngest   . . . in the family.

3
► Study the frame: Partitives, *the other one,* and *the others*

Pat Martin has four brothers.	**All** of them are married. **None** of them live in Clinton. **Two** of them live in California. **The others** live in Chicago.
She has two sisters.	**Both** of them are in college. **One** of them lives at school. **The other one** lives at home.
She has a lot of nieces and nephews.	**Most** of them live in California. **Some** of them were born there.

Partitives show what part of a whole something is.

100%	all, both
	most
	many
	some
0%	none

4
► Complete the newspaper article. Choose the correct words.
► Listen to check your work.

5
► Interview two classmates about their families. Report to the class.

Pedro has a younger brother and a younger sister. Both of them live at home.

The Martin family held their second reunion in Clinton last weekend. _____ (Many/One) of the children have moved away from Clinton, but _____ (both/all) of them showed up for the party. _____ (One/Most) of the Martins' children are married and _____ (none/all) of their grandchildren are over ten years old, so it was a noisy and happy event. Bill and Jane Martin have lived in Clinton for forty years now. They held their first family reunion eight years ago, after their youngest son moved to Chicago. "_____ (Both/Most) of our reunions have been fun," said Bill, "but this one is special because of all our new grandchildren." "_____ (The others/The other one) seemed awfully quiet," laughed Jane. We managed to talk with one grandchild, David Martin, age 4. "Great party," he assured us. _____ (The others/The other one) were all too busy to comment.

13. I see from your résumé. . .

Bill Dow is interviewing Doug Lee for a job as the director of a recreation program for teenagers. Mr. Dow runs the Community Services Agency.

1

Mr. Dow Mr. Lee, I see from your résumé that you've had a lot of experience in sales.

Doug Yes, my parents have a store. They sell housewares. I used to work there after school.

Mr. Dow Well, what kind of work have you done with adolescents?

Doug I taught swimming for a couple of summers at camp. A lot of the campers were in their early teens. Then I taught high school physical education, and I've been a guidance counselor in the Seattle public school system for the last three years.

Mr. Dow Why are you thinking of leaving your present job?

Doug Well, I enjoy counseling, but I miss athletics. This job would give me a chance to do both of them. And I feel, too, that I'm ready for a change. I've lived in Seattle my whole life.

Mr. Dow So you think you'd like living in Chicago?

Doug Very much. I've always wanted to live here.

Mr. Dow Well, Mr. Lee, you seem to have some good qualifications for the job. We're interviewing all this week, so I'll let you know in ten days or so. While you're here, I'd also like you to meet . . . (*Knock at the door*)

2. Figure it out

Say *True, False,* or *It doesn't say.*

1. Doug used to teach swimming.
2. Doug has worked with teenagers before.
3. Doug is a physical education teacher now.
4. Doug taught physical education for three years.
5. Doug likes sports.
6. Mr. Dow will call or write Doug in about ten days.
7. Mr. Dow is going to interview two other people for the job.

3. Listen in

Kate Simmons is a social worker at the Community Services Agency. Read the questions below. Then listen to the conversation and answer the questions.

1. How long has Kate worked at the Community Services Agency?
2. How long have Kate and Doug known each other?
3. Where did they meet?

14. Your turn

Here's a page from the Clinton High School Yearbook of twenty years ago. One of these people became a firefighter, one a teacher, and one an international spy.

Read about the people, and then work in groups to guess their professions. Discuss the reasons for their choices. Read the conversation before you begin.

A I think Phyllis became a teacher.
B Why?
A Because she's always liked being with people.
B I see what you mean. And she's wanted to travel since she was in high school. Teachers have long vacations.

Phyllis Sandler

Awards and Activities:
President—Great Books Club
Sarah Davis Science Award
Best Quality: Good conversationalist
Likes: People, people, people
Dislikes: Staying up late at night
Ambition: To visit a new country every year
People say:
"She's got a great sense of humor, even about herself."
"She's extremely patient—she explained chemistry to me."

David Simon

Awards and Activities:
Marathon champion
Secretary—Great Books Club
Best Quality: Fantastic memory
Likes: Learning about new things
Dislikes: Making conversation with people he doesn't know
Ambition: To save money to buy a small country house
People say:
"He's incredibly well organized. I always borrowed his notes." "He seems shy, but he's fun."

Melina Spanos

Awards and Activities:
Best Actress
President—French Club
Best Quality: Common sense
Likes: New people, new places
Dislikes: Being alone
Ambition: To retire early and write a book
People say:
"She's a great listener. People always tell her their problems . . . and she never repeats anything." "She feels comfortable in the most difficult situations."

How to say it

Practice the words. Then practice the conversation.

talked	studied	started
[t]	[d]	[əd]

A Have you talked to Mary?
B Yes, I talked to her last night.
A Has she started her music class?
B Yes, she started it last week.
A Has she studied music before?
B Well, she studied piano when she was younger.

15.

A Changing Work Force

Before you read this article, look at exercise 1. Try to guess the answers. Then read the article to see if you were right.

Is the work force changing in American life? According to statistics, America's skilled white-collar work force has overtaken the ranks of skilled blue-collar workers for the first time. Those who worry that America is becoming a nation of lawyers may have some evidence: There are now 1.4 lawyers for every farmer, whereas twenty-five years ago there were 4.5 farmers for every lawyer. Other occupations on the rise are computer analysts, doctors, police officers, and psychologists.

While women have shown steady advancement and upward mobility, their share of jobs in traditionally male roles is still relatively low. For example, the proportion of women doctors is less than one-third, while the percentage of women nurses (a typically female vocation) is still about 90%. Women represent only 3% of firefighters, 27% of veterinarians, and 15% of police officers.

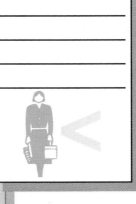

Certain occupations have declined overall in recent years. The number of jobs held by barbers, elevator operators, and farmers has been steadily shrinking. Other occupations with decreasing numbers: rail workers, tailors, and English professors.

1. Complete the tables below. Use these occupations:

nurses
police officers
tailors
doctors
elevator operators
rail workers
firefighters

English professors
computer analysts
barbers
psychologists
veterinarians
farmers
lawyers

WOMEN AT WORK

Women at work represent less than 50% of:

_____
_____
_____
_____

Women at work represent more than 50% of:

_____

JOBS ON THE RISE

Occupations that are growing:

_____
_____
_____
_____

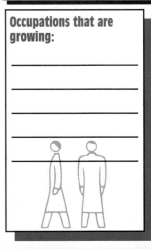

JOBS IN DECLINE

Occupations that are decreasing:

_____
_____
_____
_____

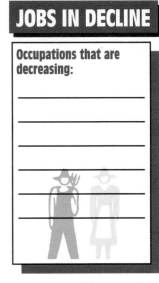

2. In your country, are there any jobs held mostly by men? Mostly by women? Is the situation changing? In what ways?

PREVIEW

FUNCTIONS/THEMES	LANGUAGE	FORMS
Give an opinion	I've heard it's not that great. It's supposed to be excellent. Was it any good? I thought so. I didn't think so.	
Talk about plans	We're thinking of going to the Picasso exhibit. I haven't seen it./I've already seen it./I've never heard of it./I haven't seen it yet. Why don't you join us? I'd like to, but I might have to work. I'd like to, but I might not be in town.	The present perfect: negative statements The present perfect with *already, never,* and *not . . . yet* The present perfect vs. the simple past tense *Might* and *might not*
Talk about things you've done and haven't done	Have you been to a sumo match yet? I went to one last night. I haven't been to one yet, but I might go tomorrow.	The present perfect vs. the simple past tense
Make suggestions	Why don't you see the new play at the Orpheum?	

Preview the conversations.

Are you going to be around this weekend?

Yes, I think so.

Oh, I've already seen it.

Wynton Marsalis

in concert at

The Green Door

Tues. through Sun.

shows at 9 & 11 p.m.

For ticket information, call 555-2243

Read the ad. Then continue the conversation between Bob and Carol.

Bob

You have two tickets to the Wynton Marsalis concert for Saturday night. Invite Carol to go with you. If she's already seen the concert, ask her opinion of it.

Carol

You went to the Wynton Marsalis concert last night and really enjoyed it. Bob has two tickets. Decide if you want to go again. If not, suggest a student in the class that Bob can invite.

16. Some of us are getting together.

 Some friends are making plans for the weekend.

A

Claire Anything exciting going on this weekend?

Janet Oh, look, Wynton Marsalis is in town.

Charlie Who's Wynton Marsalis? I've never heard of him.

Janet What? He's one of the greatest jazz musicians in the world!

Claire The tickets must cost a fortune. Are there any good movies?

Janet Well, there's a classic film festival. They're showing *La Dolce Vita*. It's supposed to be excellent.

Claire I've never seen it, but I'd like to. Why don't we go Saturday night?

Charlie I've already seen it.

Claire You have?

Charlie I just saw it the night before last.

Claire Was it any good?

Charlie I thought so. I think it's Fellini's best film.

B

Janet Let's see what's playing at the State. Oh, look . . . it's a James Bond movie. It's supposed to be really good.

Claire Fine with me. Charlie?

Charlie We could go dancing.

Janet Listen, I think we'll have to talk later. I've got to go now.

Claire Are you free on Saturday night?

Greg I might not be in town. I'm not sure yet. A friend invited me to visit him in Boston.

Claire Well, some of us are getting together, and I thought you might want to come too.

Greg What are you thinking of doing?

Claire We haven't decided yet for sure. We might go dancing, but we'll probably go see the James Bond movie that's playing at the State.

Greg Oh, I haven't seen it yet.

Claire Well, come with us then.

Greg Sure, if I'm in town. I'll call you and let you know.

Figure it out

1. Listen to the conversations. Then choose *a, b,* or *c.*

1. a. Janet has heard of Wynton Marsalis.
   b. Janet hasn't heard of Wynton Marsalis.
   c. Both Janet and Charlie have heard of Wynton Marsalis.

2. a. Janet wants to see the James Bond movie.
   b. Charlie wants to see the James Bond movie.
   c. Both Janet and Charlie want to see the James Bond movie.

3. a. Greg is going to be in town on Saturday night.
   b. Greg might be in town on Saturday night.
   c. Greg isn't going to be in town on Saturday night.

2. Listen again and say *True, False,* or *It doesn't say.*

1. Wynton Marsalis is a famous jazz musician.
2. The tickets to the Wynton Marsalis concert are probably expensive.
3. Charlie liked *La Dolce Vita*.
4. Janet has seen *La Dolce Vita*.
5. Claire and her friends are going dancing Saturday night.
6. Greg doesn't want to see the James Bond movie.
7. Greg is going to call Claire later.

3. Find another way to say it.

1. I don't know who he is.   *I've never heard of him.*
2. two nights ago
3. What did you think of it?
4. I'll tell you.
5. a lot of money
6. I've heard it's really good.
7. Maybe we'll go dancing.

17. I've heard it's not that great.

▶ Two people are talking about a movie. Listen to the conversation and circle the title of the movie.

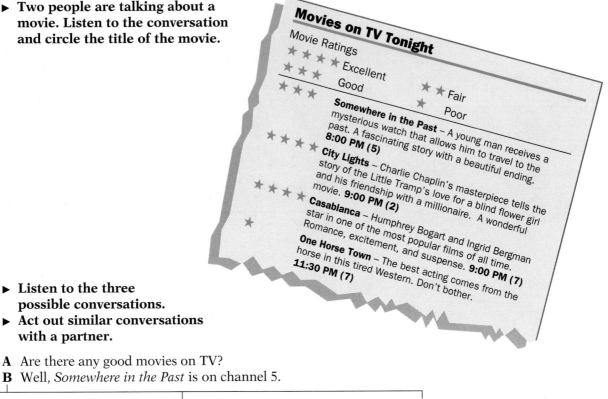

Movies on TV Tonight

Movie Ratings

★ ★ ★ ★ Excellent

★ ★ ★ Good   ★ ★ Fair

★ Poor

Somewhere in the Past – A young man receives a mysterious watch that allows him to travel to the past. A fascinating story with a beautiful ending. **8:00 PM (5)**

City Lights – Charlie Chaplin's masterpiece tells the story of the Little Tramp's love for a blind flower girl and his friendship with a millionaire. A wonderful movie. **9:00 PM (2)**

Casablanca – Humphrey Bogart and Ingrid Bergman star in one of the most popular films of all time. Romance, excitement, and suspense. **9:00 PM (7)**

One Horse Town – The best acting comes from the horse in this tired Western. Don't bother. **11:30 PM (7)**

▶ Listen to the three possible conversations.
▶ Act out similar conversations with a partner.

A Are there any good movies on TV?
B Well, *Somewhere in the Past* is on channel 5.

A Oh, it's supposed to be good. Why don't we watch that?

A Oh, not that. I've heard it's not that great. See what's on the other channels.

A I've never heard of it. Is it any good?
B It's supposed to be.

Some opinions

I've heard it's not that great.
I've heard it's exciting.
It's supposed to be excellent.
It's supposed to be boring.

▶ Listen to the two possible conversations.
▶ Work with a partner. Act out similar conversations about novels, movies, and music albums you know.

A I just read Stephen King's latest novel.
B Was it any good?

A I thought so.   **A** I didn't think so.

Other ways to say it	
What did you think of it? How did you like it?	I enjoyed it a lot. I thought it was very good.
How was it?	I didn't like it at all.

a novel

a movie

a music album

18. We're thinking of going to the Picasso exhibit.

TALK ABOUT PLANS • PRESENT PERFECT: NEGATIVE STATEMENTS • PRESENT PERFECT WITH *ALREADY, NEVER, AND NOT . . . YET* • *MIGHT* AND *MIGHT NOT*

▶ **Listen to the conversation. Which two things do the people talk about? Circle the ads.**

Picasso Exhibit

50 paintings and sculptures
May 1–28

The Modern Art Institute

KISMET

Fine Indian Cuisine

65 Park Street
555-4749

Dinner: Monday–Saturday

The Continental Club

presents

Sounds of Jamaica
live reggae music

May 8–10 • 8 PM

All the Way Home

A new play by Erica Howard

Orpheum Theater
Monday–Saturday
8:00 p.m.

CITY CENTER

Now Through May 9

**Odyssey
Dance Company**

Box office 555-5348

New World Circus

PARKSIDE STADIUM

May 6–18

10:30 AM, 2:30 PM, 7:30 PM

▶ **Listen to the two possible conversations.**
▶ **Work with a partner. Act out similar conversations about the ads.**

A We're thinking of going to the Picasso exhibit on Saturday.

B Oh, I've already seen it.
A You have?
B Yeah, I just saw it last weekend.

B Oh, I haven't seen it yet.
A Why don't you come with us then?
B Sure. I'd love to.

▶ **Study the frames: The present perfect**

Negative statements

I You We They	haven't		
		seen	it.
He She	hasn't		

Present perfect with *already,
never,* and *not . . . yet*

I've **already** seen it.

She's **never** heard of it.

I haven't seen it **yet**.

▶ **Listen to the conversation.**
▶ **Act out similar conversations with your own information.**

A Some of us are getting together Saturday night. Do you want to join us?
B Well, I'd like to, but I might have to work. I'll call you and let you know.

I might . . .

have to work.
have other plans.
be out of town.
not have time.
not be free.
not be in town.

Some of us
A couple of us
A few of us

19. Have you been to a sumo match yet?

TALK ABOUT THINGS YOU'VE DONE AND HAVEN'T DONE • PRESENT PERFECT VS. SIMPLE PAST TENSE

a sumo match

people eating at a sushi bar

a Kabuki performance

a bullet train

the Tokyo Tower

a Japanese tea ceremony

1 ▶ A travel agent and a customer are talking about things to do in Tokyo. Listen to the conversation and number the pictures in the order you hear them.

2 ▶ Listen to the two possible conversations.
▶ Imagine you are visiting Tokyo for a week. A Japanese friend is asking what you've done. Act out similar conversations using the information below.

A Have you been to a sumo match yet?

B Yes. As a matter of fact, I went to one last night.

B No. I haven't been to one yet, but I might go to one tomorrow.

> You can use *one* as a pronoun.
> go to **a** sumo match > go to **one**

THINGS TO DO IN TOKYO		
	Done?	When?
go to a sumo match	✓	last night
see a Kabuki play		maybe tomorrow night
take the bullet train		maybe tomorrow
see a tea ceremony	✓	two days ago
go to Tokyo Tower	✓	yesterday afternoon
try sushi or sashimi		maybe for dinner

3 ▶ Study the frame: The present perfect vs. the simple past tense

Use the present perfect to refer to an *unspecified* time in the past:

> **Have** you **seen** a Kabuki play?
> Yes, I**'ve** already **seen** one.

Use the simple past tense to refer to a *specific* time in the past:

> When **did** you **see** it?
> I **saw** it last night.

Use present perfect negative statements with *yet* to refer to something that didn't happen in the past but still might happen. Compare:

> I haven't seen a Kabuki play yet. (But I might see one.)
> I didn't see a Kabuki play when I was in Japan. (I'm not in Japan anymore.)

Use *yet* when you expect something to happen:

> Have you seen a Kabuki play yet?
> I haven't seen a Kabuki play yet. (But I plan to see one.)

4 ▶ **Nancy and Victor are visitors in Mexico City. Complete the conversation with the present perfect or the simple past tense of the verbs in parentheses.**
   ▶ **Listen to check your work.**

Pyramid of the Sun Teotihuacán

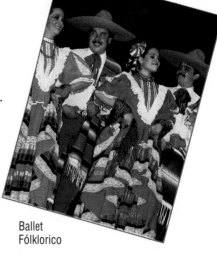

National Museum of Anthropology

Ballet Fólklorico

Nancy ___*Have you been*___ (be) to Mexico City before?
Victor Yes, I have. I _____ (come) here last year on business. But I _____ (be) only here for a few days that time, so I _____ (not/see) very much of the city on that trip.
Nancy What about this time? _____ (see) very much yet?
Victor Well, yesterday I _____ (see) the Aztec pyramids, and this morning I _____ (go) to the National Museum of Anthropology.
Nancy Oh really? I _____ (visit) that museum yesterday, and last night I _____ (see) the Ballet Fólklorico at the Palace of Fine Arts. _____ (see) the Ballet Fólklorico yet? It's a wonderful show based on traditional Mexican dances.
Victor No, I _____ (not/see) it yet, but I might go tomorrow night. I've heard it's very hard to get tickets.
Nancy Sometimes it is, but maybe you'll be lucky.

MAKE SUGGESTIONS

5 ▶ **Listen to the two possible conversations and practice them with a partner.**

A Why don't you see the new play at the Orpheum?

B I've already seen it.   **B** Good idea. I haven't seen it yet.
A You have? When did you go?
B I just went on Tuesday.

6 ▶ **Make a list of things to do in your town. Complete the chart.**
   ▶ **Work with a partner. Student A: You are a tourist. Student B: Make suggestions about things to do on the chart.**

Places to go and things to do:
Museums:
Sports:
Movies:
Music:
Other activities:

20. Can I let you know?

Laura is having a cup of coffee with her friend Wendy.

1

Wendy	Are you going out with Chuck tonight?
Laura	Uh-huh. I'm supposed to meet him at seven. What time is it now?
Wendy	Six-thirty.
Laura	You're kidding! I'd better get ready.
Wendy	Where are you going?
Laura	We haven't made up our minds yet. Maybe to a restaurant, maybe to a movie first.
Wendy	Why don't you go see *Citizen Kane* at the Classic Film Festival? It's supposed to be fantastic.
Laura	Oh, maybe we will. *Psycho* is also playing. I've heard it's really good too.
Wendy	If you like horror movies with lots of blood. Personally, I don't. Well, I really should be going. Do you want to go shopping tomorrow?
Laura	I'd like to, but I might have to go to the studio and do some work. Can I let you know first thing in the morning?
Wendy	Sure. That'll be fine. (*Rrring, rrring*)
Laura	Oh, there's the phone. It must be Chuck.
Wendy	Well, I'd better go then. Have a good time tonight.
Laura	Thanks. I'll talk to you tomorrow.

2. Figure it out

Say *True, False,* or *It doesn't say.*

1. Laura and Chuck might go to a restaurant.
2. Wendy has already seen *Citizen Kane*.
3. Wendy and Laura are thinking of going shopping tomorrow.
4. Laura is going to work tomorrow.
5. Laura hasn't seen *Psycho*.
6. Wendy will probably go to see *Psycho*.

3. Listen in

Laura is talking on the phone with Chuck. Read the statement below. Then listen to Laura's side of the conversation and choose *a, b,* or *c.*

Laura and Chuck are talking about
   a. a restaurant
   b. a class
   c. an Italian movie

21. Your turn

Work in groups. Read the poster about the Classic Film Festival. Then discuss these questions:

1. Have you ever seen any of the movies on the poster?
2. Do you like old movies? Why or why not?
3. What kinds of movies do you like the most? Why?
4. Is there a movie that most of the people in your group have seen? What did you think of the movie?

CLASSIC FILM FESTIVAL

LA DOLCE VITA
(1960)

In Federico Fellini's satire, a journalist enjoys the "sweet life" of Rome's high society, but is disturbed by it at the same time.

PSYCHO
(1960)

Alfred Hitchcock directed this thriller of murder and horror in a lonely country motel. This movie will have you on the edge of your seat.

CITIZEN KANE
(1941)

When a powerful newspaper publisher dies, a reporter tries to find out what kind of person he really was. Orson Welles both directed and starred in this brilliant piece of cinema.

RASHOMON (1951)

A crime is committed in eleventh-century Japan and is told from four different points of view. What *really* happened? This Academy Award-winning film by Akira Kurosawa brought Japanese cinema to the Western world.

How to say it

Practice the words. Then practice the conversations.

haven't [hǽvnt]   hasn't [hǽznt]   doesn't [dʌ́znt]   didn't [dídnt]

A I haven't seen the Picasso exhibit yet.
B George hasn't either. Why don't you go with him?
A He doesn't want to see it.

A I didn't have time for lunch today.
B I didn't either.

22.

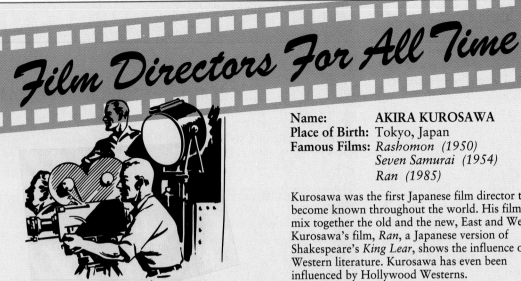

Film Directors For All Time

Name: FEDERICO FELLINI
Place of Birth: Rimini, Italy
Famous Films: *La Strada (1954)*
La Dolce Vita (1960)
Amarcord (1974)

When Fellini was a young boy, he ran away to join the circus. Even though he had to return to school, the experience greatly influenced his films, many of which are autobiographical. Fellini is known for combining realism and fantasy, often making up the story as he goes along.

Name: ALFRED HITCHCOCK
Place of Birth: London, England
Famous Films: *The Thirty-Nine Steps (1935)*
Notorious (1946)
Psycho (1960)

Hitchcock, the "Master of Suspense," made movies in both England and the United States. Many of them are about innocent people who get into trouble and can't seem to escape. Hitchcock used sound and camera techniques to heighten the feeling of panic. Many viewers enjoy trying to "spot" his short cameo appearances in all of his movies.

Name: AKIRA KUROSAWA
Place of Birth: Tokyo, Japan
Famous Films: *Rashomon (1950)*
Seven Samurai (1954)
Ran (1985)

Kurosawa was the first Japanese film director to become known throughout the world. His films mix together the old and the new, East and West. Kurosawa's film, *Ran*, a Japanese version of Shakespeare's *King Lear*, shows the influence of Western literature. Kurosawa has even been influenced by Hollywood Westerns.

Name: ORSON WELLES
Place of Birth: Kenosha, Wisconsin, U.S.A.
Famous Films: *Citizen Kane (1941)*
The Lady from Shanghai (1948)
Touch of Evil (1958)

Welles made his first and most influential film, *Citizen Kane*, when he was only 25. Considered by some film historians to be the greatest movie ever made, it is famous for unusual sound and camera techniques. Welles often acted in other directors' movies to raise money for films he wanted to direct, including a movie version of Shakespeare's *Othello*.

1. Read the article. Then scan it to find:

1. two directors known for their sound and camera techniques.
2. two directors who made films of plays by Shakespeare.
3. a director who made autobiographical films.
4. a director influenced by Hollywood Westerns.

2. Match to make sentences.

1. Hitchcock always
2. Welles frequently
3. When Fellini was a child, he
4. Kurosawa was

a. appeared briefly in his own movies.
b. acted in movies directed by other people.
c. influenced by Hollywood Westerns.
d. left home to follow a traveling circus.

FUNCTIONS/THEMES	LANGUAGE	FORMS
Talk about foreign languages	What languages do you speak? Which one do you speak the best? Do you speak English well? I hardly have an accent at all, but my grammar isn't very good.	*What* vs. *which* Adverbs
Talk about your family	Was either of your parents born in another country? They were both born here. Does she still speak Polish? She used to, but she doesn't anymore.	*Still* and *not . . . anymore*
Talk about events in the past	She's been here since she was six. He didn't know much English before he went to Canada.	Time clauses in the past: *when, before, after, as soon as,* and *since*
Tell how you met someone	How did you and your wife meet? I was teaching English at the time, and she was one of my students.	The past continuous

Preview the conversations.

1. Read the article. What are the main reasons people have immigrated to the United States?

2. Are there immigrants in your country? If so, discuss these questions with a partner:
   a. Where are they from?
   b. How long have they been in your country?
   c. Why did they come?
   d. What languages do they speak?

3. Have you ever lived in a different country (not your own)? Why did you choose to live there? Was it difficult to learn the language?

Immigration to the U.S.

Most U.S. citizens are either immigrants or descendants of immigrants. More than sixty million (60,000,000) people have left the countries of their birth and come to the United States to live. Some came for excitement and adventure. Others came to escape poverty and hunger, or political and religious oppression. Still others were brought over from Africa as slaves. These immigrants have brought their customs, languages, and foods, and have made the United States a country of great racial and ethnic diversity.

The original inhabitants of the United States were the Native American Indians. Today they make up less than 1 percent of the population.

23. What does the "K" stand for?

Luke Taylor and Maya Winston, two English teachers, are talking about their families.

A

Luke What an unusual necklace! What does the "K" stand for?

Maya "Koziol." It's my maiden name.

Luke Oh, that's Polish, isn't it?

Maya Yes. How did you know?

Luke My wife is Polish, and I've spent some time in Poland.

Maya Oh, is that where you met?

Luke No, actually, we met here in the States. I was teaching English at the time, and she was one of my students.

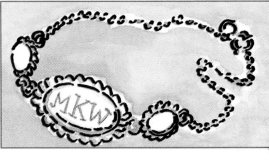

B

Maya Which language do you speak at home, English or Polish?

Luke English, most of the time. We used to speak more Polish before Stenia learned English so well.

Maya She had a good teacher.

Luke Well, she worked hard. In fact, she was one of my best students. She's also really good at languages.

Maya What languages does she speak?

Luke Polish, Russian, French, and English. She speaks English almost perfectly now. She still has a very slight accent, but you can hardly tell she's foreign.

C

Luke Was either of your parents born in Poland?
Maya Yes. They both were.
Luke Do they still speak Polish?
Maya My father used to, but he doesn't anymore. He
hasn't spoken it since my grandparents died. My
mother doesn't speak a word.
Luke How long has she been in this country?
Maya Since she was six. When she got here, she spoke
Polish, Russian, and German fluently. Unfortunately,
she forgot all of them as soon as she learned English.
Luke Do any of your relatives still live in Poland?
Maya No. They all live here now. Most of them came
over soon after my mother.

Figure it out

**1. Listen to the conversations. Then choose
a, b, or c.**

1. a. Stenia and Luke met in Poland.
   b. Stenia and Luke met in Russia.
   c. Stenia and Luke met in the U.S.

2. a. Luke and Stenia never speak Polish at home.
   b. Luke and Stenia sometimes speak Polish
      at home.
   c. Luke and Stenia always speak Polish at home.

**2. Listen again and say *True, False,* or
*It doesn't say.***

1. Koziol was Maya's name before she got married.
2. Stenia didn't know any English when she got to
   the U.S.
3. Stenia's grammar is excellent, but her accent
   is bad.
4. Maya's father still speaks Polish sometimes.
5. Maya's grandparents died a long time ago.

3. Match the words in italics with their meaning.

1. She worked *hard*.
2. Do they *still* speak Polish?
3. *Actually*, we met here.
4. *As soon as* she learned English, she forgot Polish.
5. She *hardly* speaks Polish.
6. He *used* to speak Polish, but he doesn't anymore.
7. *Unfortunately*, she's forgotten Polish.
8. We speak English *most of the time*.

a. It's too bad.
b. in the past
c. almost always
d. now
e. a lot
f. very little
g. immediately after
h. as a matter of fact

24. What languages do you speak?

1 ▶ **Listen to the job interview. Check (√) the languages the applicant says she can speak.**

____ Chinese   ____ English   ____ French
____ Italian   ____ Russian   ____ Spanish

2 ▶ **Listen to the conversation.**
    ▶ **Interview three classmates. Have similar conversations, using your own information.**

A What languages do you speak?
B French, Spanish, and English.
A Which one do you speak the best?
B French.

> *Two* languages: Which one do you speak *better*?

> *Three or more* languages: Which one do you speak *the best*?

3 ▶ **Study the frame: What vs. which**

What	languages	do you speak?
Which	language one	do you speak the best?

Use *which* instead of *what* when referring to a definite group of alternatives:
What languages (of all languages) do you speak ?
Which language (of the ones that you speak) do you speak the best?

4 ▶ **Complete the conversations with *what* or *which*.**
    ▶ **Listen to check your work.**

1   2   3

5 ▶ **Listen to the conversation.**
　 ▶ **Act out a similar conversation with a partner.**

A Do you speak English well?
B I hardly have an accent at all, but my grammar isn't very good.

Do you speak English well?
I speak it very well. (It's my native language.)
I speak it fluently, but I make some mistakes.
I speak it correctly but slowly.
I speak it very fast, but my accent is terrible.
I understand it fairly well, but I speak it poorly.
I speak it very badly.

I work very hard. = I do a lot of work.
I hardly work at all. = I do almost no work.
I hardly have an accent at all. = I have almost no accent.

Do you speak French well?

6 ▶ **Study the frame: Adverbs**

Adjectives	Adverbs
correct	correctly
perfect	perfectly
terrible	terribly
easy	easily
fantastic	fantastically
slow	slow/slowly
fast	fast
hard	hard
good	well

To form most adverbs, add *ly* to the adjective.
If the adjective ends in *le*, change the *e* to *y*.
If it ends in *y*, change the *y* to *i* and add *ly*.
If it ends in *c*, add *ally*.

7 ▶ **Rewrite the sentences evaluating these students. Use adverbs instead of adjectives.**

Donna speaks French very well.

8 ▶ **Write sentences evaluating your English ability, like the ones in exercise 7. Then compare your sentences with a partner.**

```
DEPT OF FOREIGN LANGUAGES
Name of student: Donna Clemente
Language: French
Speaking (fluency): Very good
Speaking (accuracy): Very good
Comprehension: Almost perfect

General: Donna's French is very good. It's fluent and
correct. Her understanding is almost perfect.

Name of student: Henry Wong
Language: Spanish
Speaking (fluency): A little slow
Speaking (accuracy): Good
Comprehension: Fairly good

General: Henry's Spanish is good. It's slow, but
accurate. His comprehension is fairly good.

Name of student: Anne Wood
Language: Chinese
Speaking (fluency): Excellent
Speaking (accuracy): Good
Comprehension: Good

General: Anne's Chinese is very fast and her accuracy
is good. Her comprehension is also good.
```

25. Does she still speak Polish?

1
► **Listen to the three possible conversations.**

► **Work with a partner. Act out similar conversations about your relatives.**

A Was either of your parents born in another country?

B Yes, my mother was. She was born in Poland.	**B** Yes, both of them. They were born in Poland.	**B** No. They were both born here.

A Does she still speak Polish?
B She used to, but she doesn't anymore.
A How long has she been in this country?
B Since she was six years old.

> Does she still speak Polish?
>
> Yes. She speaks it most of the time.
> Not a word. Unfortunately, she's forgotten it completely.
> No, not anymore. As soon as she came here, she stopped speaking it.

2
► **Study the frame: Time clauses in the past**

I hardly **spoke** any English	**before**	I came here.
She **stopped** speaking it	**as soon as**	she arrived.
He **learned** English	**when**	he came here.
She **forgot** how to speak it	**after**	she got here.
She's **been** here	**since**	she was six.

> Use the present perfect with *since.*

3
► **Antonio Freitas is an immigrant to Canada. Listen as he talks about himself.**

ANTONIO FREITAS 🍁 🍁 🍁

I studied English in Brazil, but unfortunately, I didn't study very hard. So when I went to Canada at the age of twenty-five, I hardly spoke any English at all.

At first I lived with other Brazilians and spoke Portuguese most of the time. One day I was doing my laundry and I needed change. The only person in the laundromat was a young Canadian woman. When I spoke to her in my broken English, she answered me in Portuguese. She was studying it at college.

Well, it was love at first sight. We got married two years later, and we've done our laundry together ever since. Now I speak English much better—almost as well as my five-year-old son.

► **Complete the sentences below. Use *when, before, after, as soon as,* or *since* in your answers.**

1. Antonio studied English *before he went to Canada* .
2. He didn't know much English _____ .
3. Antonio and his wife fell in love _____ .
4. He spoke Portuguese most of the time _____ .
5. He and his wife got married two years _____ .
6. Antonio has been in Canada _____ .

26. How did you meet?

1 ▶ **Listen to four people talk about how they met someone else. Match each conversation with the picture it describes.**

2 ▶ **Listen to the conversation.**
▶ **Act out similar conversations with a partner.**

A How did you and your wife meet?
B I was teaching English, and she was one of my students.

> She *was* teaching English.
> We *were* taking the same course.

3 ▶ **Study the frames: The past continuous**

I			
He	**was**		
She		**teaching**	English.
We			
You	**were**		
They			

Form past continuous negative statements, yes-no questions, and information questions the same way as for the present continuous, but use a past tense form of be:
 I **wasn't watching** TV.
 Were you **eating** dinner?
 What **were** you **doing**?

4 ▶ **Complete the conversations using the simple past tense or past continuous of the verbs in parentheses.**
▶ **Listen to check your work.**

1. **A** How did you meet your best friend?
   B I _____ (take) a course at the university, and she _____ (be) in my class.

2. **A** How did you meet your husband?
   B Both of us _____ (stand) in line for movie tickets, and we _____ (strike up) a conversation.

3. **A** How did you get that sunburn?
   B I was _____ (lie) on the beach, and I _____ (fall) asleep!

4. **A** How did you get interested in Japanese art?
   B I (live) _____ in Japan, and a friend _____ (introduce) me to it.

5. **A** How did you miss your plane?
   B Well, I _____ (talk) on the phone, and I _____ (not/hear) them announce the flight.

6. **A** How did you get that ugly stain on your shirt?
   B Oh, I (eat) _____ an ice cream cone, and it _____ (drip) all over!

2. I guess my mind was somewhere else.

Laura and Chuck are getting a bite to eat after seeing a movie.

1

Laura What a great movie! Wasn't it funny when he forgot her name?

Chuck Hmmm . . . I don't remember that part.

Laura It was one of the funniest parts of the movie!

Chuck I guess my mind was somewhere else.

Laura You were thinking about the interview again, weren't you?

Chuck I just can't seem to get it out of my mind. I really want that job, Laura.

Laura I know you do.

Chuck Mr. Dow seemed to think I was qualified. I can't figure out why I haven't heard yet. It's been nearly two weeks since I had the interview.

Laura Well, they said it would be about ten days. Listen, if you're so anxious to find out, why don't you call them and ask if they've made a decision yet?

Chuck Oh, I'm sure they'll let everyone know as soon as they've decided.

Laura Well, relax then. Let's think about what we're going to order. What's good here?

Chuck They used to have this great onion soup, but I don't see it anywhere on the menu.

Laura Maybe they don't serve it anymore. Here comes the waiter. Let's ask him.

2. Figure it out

Say *True, False,* or *It doesn't say.*

1. Chuck had a job interview almost two weeks ago.
2. Someone else got the job.
3. Chuck watched the movie very carefully.
4. Laura enjoyed the movie.
5. Chuck is unemployed.
6. Chuck has been to the restaurant before.

3. Listen in

The waiter is taking Laura and Chuck's order. Read the statements below. Then listen to the conversation and choose *a* or *b*.

1. The restaurant might be out of _____ .
   a. onion soup
   b. chicken soup

2. The last time Chuck ate at the restaurant _____ .
   a. the waiter was already working there
   b. the waiter wasn't working there yet

28. Your turn

The Karras family immigrated to the United States from Greece many years ago. Here's a page from their scrapbook. When do you think these photographs were taken? What do you think has happened to the family during the five generations shown in these pictures? Work in groups and make up a history of the Karras family.

Nicholas Karras and his youngest son, George, In Athens, Greece, a year before the family moved to the U.S.

The Karras brothers in the U.S.: Nicholas Jr., Gus, and George.

Helen Karras, daughter of George, is the first Karras to graduate from college.

Helen and her daughter, Christina.

Christina, her husband Alex, and their daughter Anna.

Anna visiting Athens, Greece.

How to say it

Practice the phrases. Then practice the conversation.

both of them [bóθəvəm]   some of them [sáməvəm]   all of them [ɔ́ləvəm]

A Do your parents speak Greek?
B Yes, both of them do. They were born in Greece.
A What about your brothers and sisters?
B Some of them speak Greek to my parents, but all of them speak English very well too.

29. THE FIRST AMERICANS

When did the first immigrants reach America? Scientists disagree on the date, but some say it may be much earlier than anyone thought.

> The original Americans, called "Indians" by Columbus, were the descendants of immigrants. Do you know where they came from and when they first arrived in the Americas?

When Columbus "discovered" America in 1492, he found people already living there. Thinking he had landed in the East Indies, he called these people "Indians." But *they* didn't call themselves "Indians." Stretching from the top of North America to the tip of South America were many different groups, each with its own name and way of life.

Many scientists believe that the ancestors of these people migrated to America from Asia about 11,500 years ago. At the time, the northern half of the earth was covered in ice; a lot of the land that is now under water, was then dry land. Experts believe that people from Siberia followed the animals that they hunted and traveled to Alaska over land that is now a 50-mile body of water called the Bering Strait.

When did these people migrate to the New World? This is a difficult question to answer exactly. Archeologists look for clues in the earth by digging for the remains of these early peoples. Along with bones from humans and animals, they uncover pieces of pottery, tools, and even the remains of campfires. Then they use a special technique, called radiocarbon dating, to figure out the age of these artifacts by measuring the amount of radioactive carbon in them.

Recently, archeologists have discovered clues at digs in both North and South America that lead them to believe that humans first migrated to the New World not 11,500 years ago, but much earlier—20,000 or even 50,000 years ago. These discoveries are causing a lot of excitement and controversy among experts. Two of the most interesting sites are in Chile and Brazil.

In Monte Verde, Chile, scientists working at a dig found well-preserved artifacts including stone tools and wooden bowls. They also found a human footprint and the remains of a dwelling that is very similar to a type found in Siberia. Scientists estimate that humans lived in this place 12,500 years ago. Archeologists are now working on another site that may be almost 33,000 years old.

Most of the controversy about early settlements is over the site uncovered in Pedra Furada, Brazil. Archeologist Niéde Guidon found cave paintings dating back 12,000 years. But she also uncovered charcoal from old campfires and stone tools that she believes are at least 30,000 and maybe more than 50,000 years old. Radiocarbon testing supports her findings, but some scientists still have doubts. They say that the charcoal could be from general fires in the area and not from campfires, and the "tools" could be pieces of naturally formed rock. Guidon defends her findings and even comes up with a new idea of how the early settlers got to America—they may have traveled directly from Asia to South America in boats.

What will be uncovered next? Only time will tell . . .

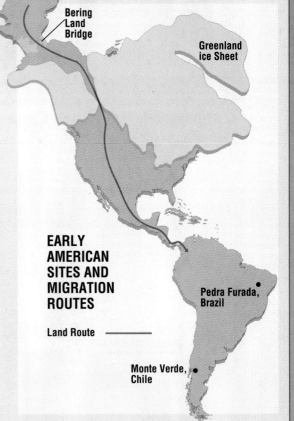

EARLY AMERICAN SITES AND MIGRATION ROUTES

Land Route ———

Bering Land Bridge

Greenland ice Sheet

Pedra Furada, Brazil

Monte Verde, Chile

---

1. Read the article. Then match these words with their definitions.

1. remains
2. artifacts
3. digs
4. dwelling
5. settlers

a. house or other place where people live
b. sites being explored by archeologists
c. tools or other objects made by humans
d. people who come to live permanently in a new place
e. parts of something that are left after most of it has been destroyed

2. Discuss these questions.

1. Where did the first American immigrants come from?
2. Why is there so much disagreement about early settlements at the site at Pedra Furada?
3. Give two possible theories about how the first settlers got to America.

Review of units 1–4

1

▶ Debbie, Brian, and Jenny are guests at Meg and Jim's wedding reception in Boston. Complete Debbie's part of the conversation.

▶ Work in groups of three. Act out similar conversations.

Debbie _____

Brian Oh, hi, Debbie. Nice to see you, too. I hear you just got back from San Francisco.

Debbie _____

Brian No, but I'd like to go there. Everyone says it's a beautiful city. By the way, have you met Jenny?

Debbie _____

Brian Debbie, this is Jenny. Jenny's from Denver.

Debbie _____

Jenny Nice to meet you, too.

Debbie _____

Jenny I'm a photographer.

Debbie _____

Jenny Well, I used to work for a magazine, but I just opened my own studio.

Debbie _____

Jenny I just met Jim today, but I've known Meg since we were in college. We were both studying fine arts and we got to be friends.

2

▶ Imagine you're at the wedding reception. Strike up a conversation with someone you know. Use one of the sentences below or your own information. Keep the conversation going.

I hear you got a new job.   *I hear you just got back from . . .*
I hear you're planning to . . .   *I hear you started your own business.*

3

▶ Work with a partner. You are both guests at the wedding. Play these roles.

Student A   You live in Boston. Find out how Student B knows Meg and Jim and if Student B has been to Boston before. If not, invite him or her to go sightseeing tomorrow.

Student B   Answer Student A's questions. You're a friend of Jim's. You've never been to Boston before, and you'll be there for two more days. You'd like to go sightseeing, but you might be busy tomorrow with friends.

4

▶ Meg, the bride, is dancing with her uncle at the reception. Listen to their conversation and say *True* or *False*.

1. Meg's uncle hasn't met Jim yet.
2. Meg and Jim went to the same university.
3. Meg works for an eye doctor now.

5 ▶ Here are some other conversations taking place at the reception. Work with a partner. Say each conversation in a different way, using the words in parentheses.

1. **A** Do you two know each other? (met)
   B No, I don't believe we've met. (have)
   A *Have you two met?*
   B *No, I don't believe we have.*

2. **A** When did meet Meg? (How long)
   B Two years ago. (for)

3. **A** How long have you lived here? (always)
   B Since I was five. Before that I lived in Korea. (used to)

4. **A** Have you known Jim long? (When)
   B I've known him since we were in college. (met)

5. **A** Have you visited Hong Kong? (ever been)
   B No, but people say it's an exciting city. (heard)

6. **A** Have you always lived in Boston? (a long time)
   B No, I've only lived here for a month. (moved)

6 ▶ Imagine you're at the wedding reception. Strike up a conversation with someone you don't know. Use one of the sentences in the box or your own ideas. Keep the conversation going.

> That's an interesting necklace.
> Are you from Boston?
> How do you know Meg and Jim?
> Have you tried these appetizers?
>   They're delicious.

7 ▶ Jenny is in her hotel room in Boston after the reception. She's calling Phil, an old friend. Complete her conversation with the words in parentheses. Use the present perfect or the simple past tense.
▶ Listen to check your work.

. . . Hi, Phil! This is Jenny. I'm here in Boston. . . . I _____ (be) here for two days. . . . I _____ (get) here on Friday. . . . Well, yesterday I _____ (see) the Salvador Dalí exhibit at the Museum of Fine Arts, and today I _____ (go) to a wedding. . . . Meg Wilson and Jim Harris . . . . No, I don't think you know them. Meg and I _____ (go) to college together. . . . No, I _____ (not/see) Beth yet, but I just _____ (speak) to her on the phone a few minutes ago. We're thinking of getting together tomorrow night. Maybe you'd like to join us. . . . We _____ (not/decide) yet. . . . Oh, I _____ (already/see) it . . . . That's a good idea. I _____ (not/be) to the theater for months . . . . I'll call Beth back and ask her if she wants to see it. . . .

8 ► Beth is talking on the phone with Jenny. Which play are they talking about? Listen to Beth's side of the conversation and circle the ad.

WAITING FOR SUMMER
by Michael Jeffreys
WILBUR THEATER
Monday–Saturday
8:00 p.m.

Lisa Stone
and
Keith Bolin
in
The White Rose
Charles Street
Theater
Tuesday–Saturday
8:00 p.m.

THAT
WONDERFUL
NIGHT
starring Elizabeth Hudson
Orpheum Theater
Monday–Saturday, 7:30 p.m.

9 ► A friend calls and asks if you'd like to see the play *Waiting for Summer* on Saturday night. Choose one of the roles below and act out the conversation with a partner.

Role A: You've never heard of the play. At first you're not sure you can go because you have an exam on Monday, but you want to do something interesting this weekend.

Role B: You've heard that the play is really good, but you might not be free on Saturday night. Give a reason why you might be busy.

Role C: You've already seen the play. Suggest doing something else.

10 ► Jenny and Beth are waiting for Phil in front of the theater. Complete Beth's part of the conversation.

Beth _____

Jenny No. I don't work for the magazine anymore. I have my own studio now.

Beth _____

Jenny For about a month. I'm really excited about it. I've always wanted to have my own business. But tell me, what's new with you?

Beth _____

Jenny Really? How did you meet him?

Beth _____

Jenny Was he born in Italy?

Beth _____

Jenny Since high school, huh? Does he still speak Italian?

Beth _____

Jenny No kidding. *You* speak Italian? Do you speak it well?

Beth _____

11 ► Imagine you're talking to a friend you haven't seen for a long time. Talk about your family, your job, things you've done, or people you've met.

12 ▶ It's the day after Phil went to the theater with Jenny and Beth. He's talking to his friend Lou. Put the conversation in order.
▶ Listen to check your work.
▶ Act out a similar conversation with a partner.

____ Oh, I haven't seen it, but I've heard it's very good. How did you like it?

____ I've always wanted to see one of his plays. Where's it playing?

____ Well, maybe I'll go this weekend. I might ask Marilyn to go.

_1_ Have you seen any good movies lately?

____ Oh, she's already seen it. I saw her at the theater last night.

____ No, but I just saw a play last night—*Waiting for Summer*.

____ It was excellent. Michael Jeffreys wrote it, you know.

____ At the Wilbur Theater.

13 ▶ Work with a partner. Tell your partner about a movie, play, or some other event you went to recently. Answer your partner's questions.

14 ▶ Work with the same partner. Talk about your plans for next weekend.
▶ Say what you might and might not do. Then report to the class.

Lily might ride her motorcycle.
Boris might go for a midnight swim.

15 ▶ Listen to the first part of each conversation and choose the best response.

1. a. Nice to meet you, too.
   b. Nice to see you, too.

2. a. Thanks, it's from Greece.
   b. Oh, thanks.

3. a. No, I never have.
   b. Yes, I'm going next year.

4. a. Last year.
   b. For a year.

5. a. Six months ago.
   b. For six months.

6. a. She's fine.
   b. They're both fine.

7. a. Thanks, but I've already seen it.
   b. Thanks, but I've already read it.

8. a. Where does the other one live?
   b. Where do the other ones live?

9. a. No, not anymore.
   b. No, not yet.

10. a. Yes, he speaks it poorly.
    b. Yes, he speaks it fluently.

P R E V I E W

FUNCTIONS/THEMES	LANGUAGE	FORMS
Ask for advice	Do you know of any hotels around here? Did you have anything special in mind? Just someplace clean and inexpensive. Which one is the nicest? The Harvest is the nicest, but it's also the most expensive.	Indefinite compounds with adjectives The superlative of adjectives
Ask how to get somewhere	What's the best way to get to The Harvest? You can either walk or take a bus. It's about a thirty-minute walk or fifteen minutes by bus. So, it's faster by bus.	Comparatives vs. superlatives
Ask for and give directions	Could you please tell me how to get to Toby's "Good Eats"? When you get to Yorkville, turn left. Stay on Bellair until you get to Bloor Street. You can't miss it.	Future time clauses with the simple present tense: *when, just before, just after, as soon as,* and *until*

Preview the conversations.

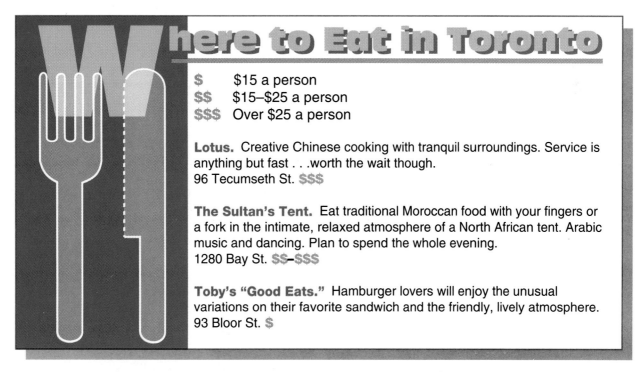

Where to Eat in Toronto

$ $15 a person
$$ $15–$25 a person
$$$ Over $25 a person

Lotus. Creative Chinese cooking with tranquil surroundings. Service is anything but fast . . .worth the wait though.
96 Tecumseth St. $$$

The Sultan's Tent. Eat traditional Moroccan food with your fingers or a fork in the intimate, relaxed atmosphere of a North African tent. Arabic music and dancing. Plan to spend the whole evening.
1280 Bay St. $$–$$$

Toby's "Good Eats." Hamburger lovers will enjoy the unusual variations on their favorite sandwich and the friendly, lively atmosphere.
93 Bloor St. $

1. Read the descriptions of three Toronto restaurants. Then choose a partner and compare the restaurants to each other. You may use these adjectives: *expensive, pricey, reasonable, cheap, relaxed, interesting,* and *lively.*
2. Now make plans with three other students to have dinner out in your town. Compare different restaurants and then decide where to go. Here are some more adjectives you may use: *close, far, small, large, crowded, romantic, exotic,* and *busy.*

30. You can't miss it.

Two tourists, Kathy and George Dupont, are looking for a place to have lunch in Toronto.

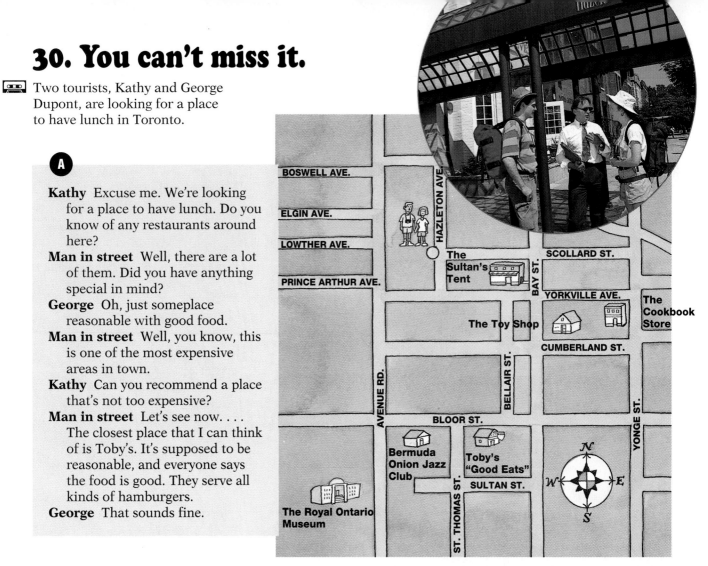

A

Kathy Excuse me. We're looking for a place to have lunch. Do you know of any restaurants around here?

Man in street Well, there are a lot of them. Did you have anything special in mind?

George Oh, just someplace reasonable with good food.

Man in street Well, you know, this is one of the most expensive areas in town.

Kathy Can you recommend a place that's not too expensive?

Man in street Let's see now. . . . The closest place that I can think of is Toby's. It's supposed to be reasonable, and everyone says the food is good. They serve all kinds of hamburgers.

George That sounds fine.

B

George Could you tell us how to get to the restaurant?

Man in street Do you know where Yorkville Avenue is?

George Yes.

Man in street Well, when you get to Yorkville, turn left. Then go one more block and turn right on Bellair. Just stay on Bellair until you get to Bloor Street. The restaurant will be right across the street. You can't miss it.

Kathy What's it called again?

Man in street Toby's "Good Eats."

Art Gallery of Ontar[io]

C

Kathy One more thing . . . what's the best way to get to the Art Gallery of Ontario?

Man in street You can either walk or take the subway.

George How far is it? My feet are killing me.

Man in street Oh, not that far. About a thirty-minute walk, I'd say.

George We'll take the subway.

Man in street Well, then after you eat, walk a couple of blocks west on Bloor and take the University subway south to St. Patrick.

Kathy Thanks a lot. You've been very helpful.

Man in street Don't mention it. Enjoy your day.

Figure it out

1. Listen to the conversations and choose the correct answers.

1. a. George and Kathy live in the neighborhood.
   b. George and Kathy don't know the neighborhood very well.

2. a. George and Kathy have walked a lot today.
   b. George and Kathy just got off the subway.

2. Listen again and say *True, False,* or *It doesn't say.*

1. George and Kathy don't want to spend a lot of money.
2. The man has eaten at Toby's many times.
3. George's feet hurt.
4. Most of the restaurants in the area are very reasonable.
5. George and Kathy are going to take the subway to the restaurant.

3. Choose *a* or *b*.

1. Do you know _____ ?
   a. where is Bloor Street
   b. where Bloor Street is

2. Could you tell us how _____ ?
   a. to get there
   b. do you get there

3. It's a _____ walk.
   a. ten-minutes
   b ten-minute

4. Stay on Bellair until _____ .
   a. you'll get to Bloor
   b. you get to Bloor

31. Do you know of any hotels around here?

1 ▶ **Read the three ads. Then listen to the conversation. Circle the ad for the hotel that the man describes.**

CONTINENTAL HOTEL
• swimming pool
• cable TV
• air conditioning
"One of the best values in the city."
740 Clark Street
555-2930

The Milburn Hotel
• Convenient location
• Reasonable rates
• Free parking
45 Bedford Avenue
555-9738

"In the heart of the city"
THE WESTGATE INN
Easy to reach by subway or bus
555-1925
273 Union Boulevard

2 ▶ **Listen to the three possible conversations.**
▶ **Work with a partner. Have similar conversations about restaurants and hotels in your town.**

A Do you know of any hotels around here?

| **B** Yes. There's one on State Street. | **B** Well, there are quite a few. Did you have anything special in mind?
A No, nothing special. Just someplace clean and inexpensive. | **B** No. I'm afraid I don't. |

a hotel	a restaurant
clean	reasonable
convenient	unusual
inexpensive	close
modern	with good food
with parking	with a nice atmosphere
	with fast service

3 ▶ **Study the frames: Indefinite compounds with adjectives**

someone	anyone	no one	everyone	**someone** important
something	anything	nothing	everything	**anywhere** interesting
someplace	anyplace	no place	everyplace	**nothing** special
somewhere	anywhere	nowhere	everywhere	**everything** good

4 ▶ **Two roommates are talking. Complete the conversation with indefinite compounds followed by adjectives when appropriate.**
▶ **Listen to a possible conversation.**

Did you do *anything special*?

A Hi! How was your day? Did you do *anything special*?
B No, _____ _____ .
A Well, did you go _____ ?
B No, _____ _____ .
A That's the TV section, isn't it? Is there _____ _____ on TV?
B _____ _____ . Just the same old shows. I've already seen _____ _____ .
A Oh, by the way, did _____ call?
B No, _____.

32. Which one is the nicest?

1 ▶ Bruce just moved into his apartment. Listen to the conversation with his neighbor, Jim, and check (√) the things they talk about.

a restaurant

a doctor

a dentist

a shoe store

a department store

a bakery

2 ▶ Listen to the three possible conversations and practice them with a partner.
▶ Look at the pictures above and act out similar conversations about your neighborhood.

A Can you recommend a nice restaurant in this neighborhood?

B Yes. I know of one.
A Is it expensive?
B No, not really.

B Well, there are three—
The Harvest, The Kitchen, and Sylvia's.
A Which one is the nicest?
B The Harvest is the nicest, but it's also the most expensive.

B No, I'm sorry, I don't know of any.

> *Two* restaurants: The Harvest is *nicer than* The Kitchen.
> *Three or more* restaurants: The Harvest is *the nicest* restaurant.

3 ▶ Study the frames: The superlative of adjectives

Sylvia's has		**fastest**	service in town.
The Harvest is	the	**most expensive**	restaurant.
The Kitchen is		**least expensive**	restaurant.
It's			**nicest**.

Some adjectives	Which one is . . .
nice	the nicest?
close	the closest?
far	the farthest?
good	the best?
bad	the worst?
expensive	the most expensive?
inexpensive	the least expensive?

4 ▶ Complete the conversation with the superlative form of the adjectives in parentheses.
▶ Listen to check your work.

A I need a new pair of shoes. Can you recommend a good shoe store?
B Well, Shoe King is _____ (good), but it's also _____ (far).
A Do you know of one that's not too far?
B Let me see. _____ (close) place I can think of is Tip Top Shoes.
A Are their shoes expensive?
B Oh no. It's _____ (inexpensive) shoe store in town. They also have _____ (large) selection.
A That sounds fine. Thanks.

33. What's the best way to get to The Harvest?

ASK HOW TO GET SOMEWHERE • COMPARATIVES VS. SUPERLATIVES

1

- **Listen to the conversation.**
- **Work with a partner. Act out similar conversations about places in your town.**

A What's the best way to get to The Harvest?
B You can either walk or take a bus.
A How far is it?
B Oh, it's about a thirty-minute walk or fifteen minutes by bus.
A So, it's faster by bus.

Some means of transportation	Some times
walk	a thirty-minute walk
take a bus	a fifteen-minute bus (subway) ride
take a subway	ten minutes by subway (bus)
drive	a two-hour drive

thirty minutes, *but* a thirty-minute walk

2

- **Study the frames: Comparatives vs. superlatives**

Before adding *-er* or *-est*:
Drop the *e* when an adjective ends in *e* (*close-closer-closest*). Double the consonant when an adjective ends in a single vowel + a consonant (*big - bigger - biggest*). Change *y* to *i* (*busy - busier - busiest*).

Adjective	Comparative form	Superlative form
fast	fast**er**	**the** fast**est**
close	clos**er**	**the** clos**est**
big	bi**gger**	**the** bi**ggest**
busy	bus**ier**	**the** bus**iest**
good	**better**	**the best**
bad	**worse**	**the worst**
far	far**ther**	**the** far**thest**
expensive	**more** expensive	**the most** expensive
inexpensive	**less** expensive	**the least** expensive

3

- **Complete the letter, using the comparative or superlative form of the adjectives in parentheses.**
- **Listen to check your work.**

December 20th

Dear Mary and Bob,

I'm really sorry I haven't written, but the holidays are the *busiest* (busy) time of the year for me at the store. The children are a lot _______ (big) than when you saw them. I think Nancy is going to be _______ (tall) one in the family very soon. Jim is one of _______ (good) students in his class. He had a little trouble with math last year, but it's a lot _______ (easy) for him now. Harry is _______ (happy) and _______ (relaxed) since he started his new job. _______ (important) thing is that the hours are _______ (short).

This has been one of _______ (bad) winters in a long time. I hope the weather gets _______ (warm) soon.

How's everything with you? Do you have plans to

4

- **Work with a partner. Find out: What is your partner's busiest day of the week? What was the happiest day of your partner's life? What was the most expensive thing your partner ever bought? What's the best book your partner ever read? What's the worst movie your partner has ever seen?**

34. When you get to Yorkville, turn left.

1 ▶ **Listen to the conversation and practice it with a partner.**

A Could you please tell me how to get to Toby's "Good Eats"?
B Sure. Do you know where Yorkville Avenue is?
A Yes, I do.
B Well, when you get to Yorkville, turn left. Then go one more block and turn right on Bellair. Stay on Bellair until you get to Bloor Street. Toby's will be right across the street. You can't miss it!
A Thanks a lot.
B Don't mention it.

> **Some places in Toronto**
>
> Toby's "Good Eats"
> The Sultan's Tent
> The Royal Ontario Museum
> Bermuda Onion Jazz Club
> The Toy Shop
> The Cookbook Store

2 ▶ **Work with a partner. Imagine you're at the corner of Hazelton and Scollard in Toronto. Ask how to get to one of the places listed in the box. Your partner will give your directions using the map on page 48.**

> **Some locations**
>
> across the street
> on the left
> about halfway down the block
> at/on the corner

3 ▶ **Study the frames: Future time clauses with** *when, just before, just after, as soon as,* **and** *until.*

Turn right You'll see the store	**when** **just before** **just after** **as soon as**	you get to Bloor.
Stay on Bellair	**until**	

> Use a simple present tense verb in time clauses that refer to future time, even when another verb in the sentence is in the future:
>
> Turn right when you get to Bloor.
> You'll pass two traffic lights before you get there.

4 ▶ **Look at the map. Imagine you're walking on First Street and a driver asks you for directions to Mama's Kitchen. Complete the conversation with appropriate time clauses.**

Driver Excuse me. How do you get to Mama's Kitchen from here?

You Stay on First Street *until you get to* Market Street. _____ Market, turn right. Then go straight ahead _____ Baker Street. _____ Baker, you'll see a travel agency. _____ the travel agency, get in the left lane. Turn left on Baker at the light. Mama's Kitchen is near the end of the block on the left.

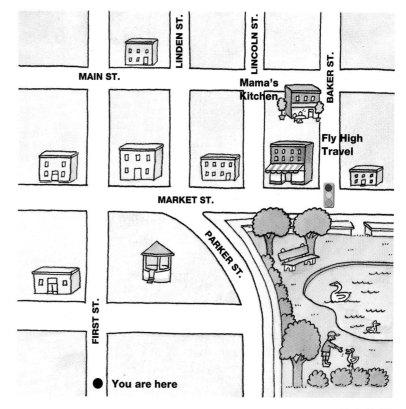

35. You can't keep them home anymore.

Laura's mother, Mrs. Enders, is shopping for a gift for Laura's sister at Lee's Housewares.

① 1

Mrs. Lee	May I help you find something, or are you just looking?
Mrs. Enders	I'm trying to find something for my daughter. She just moved into a new apartment.
Mrs. Lee	Did you have anything special in mind?
Mrs. Enders	Something practical. I know she needs a lot of things. . . . Maybe a nice pot.
Mrs. Lee	Well, these are the best pots we carry. Feel how heavy this one is.
Mrs. Enders	I'm afraid it's a bit too heavy. I have to carry it with me on the plane.
Mrs. Lee	Well, they also come in smaller sizes. I've had some for ten years, and they're still like new.
Mrs. Enders	I'll take this smaller one. Do you accept credit cards?
Mrs. Lee	No, I'm sorry, we don't. We take either cash or a check with ID. Where does your daughter live?
Mrs. Enders	In Chicago. In fact, both of my daughters live in Chicago. You know kids nowadays. You can't keep them home anymore.
Mrs. Lee	It's true. My son is thinking of moving to Chicago too, as a matter of fact. He had an interview there. Now he's waiting to hear if he got the job.
Mrs. Enders	Who do I make the check out to?
Mrs. Lee	Lee's Housewares.

2. Figure it out

Say *True, False,* or *It doesn't say.*

1. Mrs. Enders is going to Chicago.
2. Mrs. Lee's son is moving to Chicago.
3. Laura's sister is looking for an apartment.
4. Mrs. Enders buys the heaviest pot.
5. Mrs. Enders has two daughters.
6. Mrs. Enders gives Mrs. Lee cash.

3. Listen in

Mrs. Enders also needs a bathroom scale. Read the statement below. Then listen to the conversation and choose *a* or *b*.

Ace Hardware is _____ .
a. before The Shoe Place
b. after The Shoe Place

36. Your turn

Imagine that you live in Kyoto, Japan. Your partner is a tourist who starts a conversation with you and then asks you the questions below. Using the map, give your partner directions. You are standing on the corner of Nichioji and Shijo streets.

A *Where can I get a train to Tokyo?*
B *Walk about two blocks along Shijo Street and turn right on Horikawa Street. Then walk two blocks to Shichijo Street. The train station is on the left, near the corner of Horikawa and Shichijo.*

1. Where can I get some information about Kyoto?
2. Where can I buy some presents for my family?
3. I'd like to see a traditional Japanese play. Is there a theater near here?
4. I'd like to visit Kyoto University. Is it far from here?

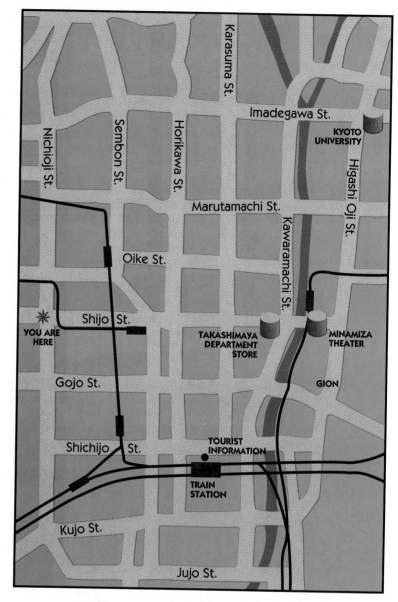

How to say it

Practice the conversation.

A How do I get to the train station from here?

B You can either drive or take a bus.

A Is it far?

B Well, it's about a ten-minute drive and about twenty minutes by bus.

Gion, the neigborhood of the Minamiza Theater

When in Japan...

Do you know the customs in Japan for greeting other people? . . . eating a meal in a restaurant? . . . tipping? . . . giving gifts? Read the article and find out.

Do you enjoy traveling to other countries? Do you like to see new sights, taste new foods, and understand how foreign cultures are different from your own? There is a proverb that goes: When in Rome, do as the Romans do. This means that it is a good idea to try to learn the customs of the place you are visiting, and then behave in a similar fashion.

If you plan to travel to Japan, it might be helpful to know some Japanese customs about public behavior, dining out, tipping, and gifts before you go.

Even though you may be familiar with pictures of people in Tokyo crowded into trains during rush hour, be aware that people in Japan value their personal space. You might be used to touching someone on the arm or giving a pat on the shoulder, but do not do this in Japan. You greet a person by bowing or nodding, or sometimes by shaking hands. If you want to get the attention of a waiter or a salesperson, put your hand out in front of you, palm down, and wave it up and down. Don't confuse this with the gesture for "No," which is to wave your right hand back and forth in front of your face, with your palm facing left.

When dining out, before you start a meal, you will be given a basket with a hot towel in it. Use this towel to wipe your hands and then put it back in the basket. A napkin is not usually used. Be sure to wait until the older people at your table pick up their chopsticks before you begin eating.

You will find rice served at every meal. Always alternate a bite of rice with a bite of the side dishes. Don't eat just one dish at a time; this is considered rude. Drink soup directly from the bowl, but don't finish your soup before eating other dishes; it should accompany the entire meal.

When it is time to pay the bill, if the other person has invited you to dinner, let that person pay. If you wish to treat, be the first one to pick up the bill. Don't spend time checking over the bill. Honesty is very important and you can assume that the numbers are correct. And your change will not be counted out in front of you; it will just arrive on a tray. There is no need to leave a tip, for tipping is almost unheard of in Japan.

You will find that gifts are important. You should bring something when you visit, but it shouldn't be too expensive or your host will be uncomfortable. Avoid giving four of anything—the word for "four" is similar to the word for "death." All gifts, even money, should be wrapped, but your host will probably not open the gift in front of you, in order to show that the act of giving is more important than the actual gift. Use both hands when you give or receive a gift.

Remember, people always appreciate tourists who respect their customs. Happy traveling!

1. **What advice would you give to a visitor to Japan about:**

1. greeting or meeting someone for the first time.
2. eating in a restaurant.
3. paying the bill and tipping.
4. giving gifts.

2. **How do these Japanese customs differ from customs in other countries you know?**

FUNCTIONS/THEMES	LANGUAGE	FORMS
Express an obligation	I have to be at a meeting at noon. I'm supposed to pick up the kids at 5:00. I'd better go.	*Have to* and *be supposed to* *Had better* Two-word verbs
Leave a message with someone	If my son calls, tell him to be ready at six.	
Make a request	Could you explain them to me?	*Could*
Ask a favor of someone Offer to do someone a favor	Would you do me a favor? Would you please give this note to Mary for me? Would you explain this to me? Oh, I'll call her for you. I'll introduce you to him.	*Would* Indirect objects with *to* and *for* Direct and indirect objects
Ask for help	Could you show me how to work the VCR? I'm not sure how to record.	Question words with infinitives
Call an office	May I tell her who's calling? Would you have her call me when she gets back?	

Preview the conversations.

> For _Ms. Clark_
> Date _10/14_   Time _2:00_
> **WHILE YOU WERE OUT**
> M r. _John Willard_
> From _The Wheaton Company_
> Phone No. _555–3456_
> ☑ TELEPHONED   ☐ URGENT
> ☑ PLEASE CALL
> ☐ WILL CALL AGAIN   ☐ WANTS TO SEE YOU
> ☐ RETURNED YOUR CALL ☐ CAME TO SEE YOU
> Message _He'll be out from_
> _2:30 to 3:00_

Read the message form. Then choose a partner and act out the conversations in the two situations below. Play the role of John Willard or Anne Jenkins. End the second conversation any way you wish.

1. John Willard calls Joan Clark, the president of Clark Associates, at 2:00 P.M. Ms. Clark is at a meeting. Her assistant, Anne Jenkins, takes the message on the message form.

2. At 4:30 P.M., Mr. Willard calls again because Ms. Clark hasn't called him back. Ms. Clark just got back, and Ms. Jenkins gave her the message as soon as she came in.

38. Do you know what time it is?

It's a busy day for Anne Jenkins, an administrative assistant at Clark Associates.

A

Joan Anne, do you know what time it is?

Anne It's five to twelve.

Joan Listen, would you do me a favor? I have a lunch meeting with Alex Post, and I'm supposed to be there at noon. Would you call him for me and tell him I'm on my way?

Anne Sure.

Joan Thanks a lot. Oh, and one more thing . . . if my son Johnny calls, tell him to be ready at six. I'll pick him up on my way home.

Anne O.K.

Joan Oh, wait, I'd better call my husband. He might think *he's* supposed to pick up Johnny.

Anne Why don't you just go? I'll call him for you.

Joan Do you mind?

Anne No, not at all.

Joan Thanks so much. By the way, did you send Mr. Post our sales report?

Anne Yes. I sent it to him last week.

Joan I can always count on you, Anne. Well, I'm off. I should be back no later than three.

B

Receptionist Post, Cramden, and Lowe.

Anne Alex Post, please. (*Rrring, rrring*)

Mr. Post's assistant Mr. Post's office.

Anne May I speak to Mr. Post, please?

Mr. Post's assistant May I tell him who's calling?

Anne Yes, this is Anne Jenkins from Clark Associates.

C

Anne Good afternoon, Clark Associates.
Donald May I please speak to Ms. Clark?
Anne I'm sorry, she's not in the office.
Donald When do you expect her back?
Anne She should be back by three. Would you like to leave a message?
Donald This is Donald Todd. Would you please have her call me? My number is 555-4433. It's quite important.
Anne I'll give her the message as soon as she gets in.
Donald Thank you.
Office worker Uh . . . excuse me, can I ask you a question? Could you show me how to work the photocopier? I'm not sure where to put the paper.
Anne Sure, I'd be glad to.
Office worker Maybe you could explain the instructions to me. I can't seem to figure them out.

D

Joan Well, see you tomorrow.
Anne I'd better go, too. Thursday's my daughter's birthday, and I want to get her a new robe.
Joan I think you're going to have to buy it for her tomorrow. The stores are closing in fifteen minutes.
Anne Oh, no! You're right. I guess I lost track of the time.

Figure it out

1. Listen to the conversations. Then choose *a* or *b*.

1. a. Joan is going to pick up her son.
   b. Joan's husband is supposed to pick up their son.

2. a. Joan will be back at three.
   b. Joan expects to be back before three.

2. Listen again and say *True, False,* or *It doesn't say.*

1. Joan is going to be late for her meeting.
2. Joan's son might call.
3. Donald Todd called before three.
4. The office worker has used the photocopier before.
5. Anne has worked at Clark Associates for a long time.
6. Anne always knows what time it is.

3. Match.

1. Would you please have her   a. me that question.
2. Tell my son   b. for you.
3. I gave it   c. call me.
4. I'm not sure where   d. to you.
5. I bought it   e. that question to me.
6. He explained   f. to put the paper.
7. He asked   g. to call me.

39. I'm supposed to pick up the kids.

1 ▶ Rita just started a job as a receptionist. Her boss is explaining the job on the first day. Listen and check (√) Rita's responsibilities on the list.

Both *I have to* and *I'm supposed to* show obligation, but *I'm supposed to* can also show that something was planned or arranged:

I **have to** be at a meeting at noon. (So I'm going.)
I'm **supposed to** be at a meeting now. (But I'm not there.)

▶ Now use the checklist to talk about Rita's job. Use *has to* and *is supposed to*.

Rita is supposed to be at work at 8:30 A.M.

√ be at work at 8:30 A.M.
make coffee
type letters
make photocopies
distribute mail
turn on the lights and photocopier
send faxes
answer phones and take messages

2 ▶ Listen to the conversation.
▶ Act out similar conversations using the information in the appointment book.

A Do you know what time it is?
B It's ten to five.
A Oh, I'd better go. I'm supposed to pick up my kids at 5:00.

When the object of a two-word verb is a noun, the verb can usually be separated or not separated:

Pick the kids **up**. **Turn** the copier **on**.
Pick up the kids. **Turn on** the copier.

When the object of a two-word verb is a pronoun (it, them, her, him, etc.) the verb must be separated:

Pick them **up**.
Turn it **on**.

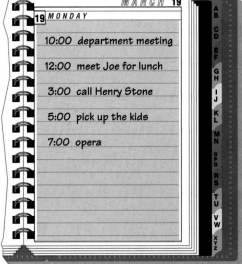

MARCH 19

19 *MONDAY*

10:00 department meeting

12:00 meet Joe for lunch

3:00 call Henry Stone

5:00 pick up the kids

7:00 opera

3 ▶ Work with a partner. Talk about obligations you have today and tomorrow.

I'm supposed to meet my sister at six.
I have to go the dentist tomorrow.

LEAVE A MESSAGE WITH SOMEONE

4 ▶ Joan Clark left messages with Anne Jenkins for these people. Match the people with the messages.

a. Tell her I'll call her back after three.
b. Tell him to come fix the photocopier as soon as he can.
c. Tell her I'll pick up the airline tickets tomorrow.

the travel agent   the repairman   my mother

5 ▶ Work with a partner. Give your partner messages for people who might call you.

If my sister calls, tell her to meet me at six.

40. Would you explain this to me?

1 ▶ What requests are these people making? Complete the conversations with the phrases in the box.
  ▶ Listen to check your work.
  ▶ Practice the conversations with a partner.

a. explain them to me
b. send it to him
c. give them back to her
d. introduce me to him

2 ▶ Look at the pictures and complete the conversations with the phrases in the box.
  ▶ Listen to check your work.
  ▶ Practice the conversations with a partner.

a. give this note to Mary for me
b. call a taxi for me
c. buy me a copy of *Time* on your way home
d. explain this math problem to me

3 ▶ Work with a partner. Ask him or her to do you a favor. Use your own ideas of the favors in the box below.

Some favors

Get a bottle of aspirin **for me** at the drugstore.
Buy a newspaper **for me** when you go out.
Make an appointment **for me** with Dr. Janik.

Lend your book **to me** when you're done with it.
Explain this problem **to me**.

41. Oh, I'll call her for you.

1 ▶ **Listen to the conversation and practice it with a partner.**

A I'd better call Nancy. She's expecting me in five minutes.
B Oh, I'll call her for you.

2 ▶ **Work with a partner. Look at the pictures and act out conversations like the one in exercise 1. Student A: Imagine you are the person in the picture. Student B: Offer to do Student A a favor.**

I'd better call the dentist and tell her I'm going to be late.

I'd better make some coffee or I'll fall asleep.

I'd better pick up some milk at the store. There's none left.

3 ▶ **Study the frames:**
Direct and indirect objects

	Direct object		Indirect object
Give	**the book**	to	**Joe**.
Buy	**it**	for	**him**.

	Indirect object	Direct object
Give	**Joe**	**the book**.
Buy	**him**	

Use *to* before the indirect object with these verbs:

bring	sell	take
give	send	tell
lend	show	

Use *for* before the indirect object with these verbs:

bake	find	save
build	get	
buy	make	

To + the indirect object always comes *after* the direct object of these verbs:

describe	explain	say
introduce	return	

Explain the instructions **to me**.

The indirect object always comes *before* the direct object of the verb *ask:*

He **asked me** a question.

4 ▶ **Complete the conversations, using direct and indirect object pronouns.**
▶ **Listen to check your work.**
▶ **Practice the conversations with a partner.**

1. **A** Your friend Pete looks interesting. I'd really like to meet ___*him*___.
   B Oh, I'll introduce _*you to him*_.

2. **A** I borrowed this book from Laila a month ago. I really should return _____.
   B She's in my class. I'll give _____.

3. **A** I've looked everywhere for my keys, but I can't find _____.
   B Take it easy. I'll find _____ .

4. **A** This math problem is really hard. I don't understand _____.
   B Don't worry. I'll explain _____ .

5 ▶ **Talk to your classmates. Tell them about things you'd better do or are having a problem with. Your classmates will offer to do you a favor.**

42. I'm not sure how to record.

1 **Listen to the conversation and practice it with a partner.**

A Excuse me. Could you show me how to work the VCR? I'm not sure how to record.
B Sure. I'd be glad to.
A And maybe you could explain this form to me. I don't know what to write on this line.
B I'm not sure what to write on it either.

2 ► **Study the frame: Question words with infinitives**

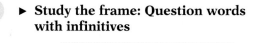

| Where do you put the paper? | |
| How do you turn on the machine? | |

| I'm not sure | **where to put** the paper. |
| I don't know | **how to turn on** the machine. |

3 ► **Work with a partner. Ask for help operating these machines. Act out conversations like the one in exercise 1.**

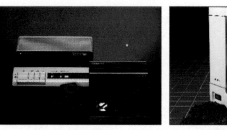

answering machine   coffee maker

photocopier   fax machine

4 ► **Listen to the conversation and practice it with a partner.**

A May I speak to Ms. Clark, please?
B May I tell her who's calling?
A This is Jim Todd.
B One moment. (*Pause*) I'm sorry. She's not in her office.

A When do you expect her back?
B She should be back by three. Would you like to leave a message?
A Yes. Could you ask her to call me? My number is 555-4433.
B I'll give her the message as soon as she gets back, Mr. Todd.

5 ► **Work with a partner. Take turns playing these roles:**

Student A Call Clark Associates and ask to speak to one of the people in the pictures.
Student B Play the role of the receptionist. Use the information below the pictures.

Mr. Gray

Mr. Gray just stepped out for a few minutes.

Ms. Chu

Ms. Chu is on vacation until next Monday.

Mr. Benowitz

Mr. Benowitz is out to lunch until two.

43. I was starting to worry.

Back in Seattle, Washington, Doug is eating dinner with his family.

1

Doug	Does anyone know what time it is?
Mr. Lee	It's exactly seven o'clock.
Doug	I'd better get going soon. Someone's supposed to come over at eight to look at the apartment.
Mrs. Lee	Well, you can't leave before you have a piece of this cake Dad made.
Doug	Hey, chocolate cake! All right!
Mr. Lee	It's in honor of your new job.
Doug	You know, I still can't believe I got it. I was starting to worry when two weeks went by with no news.
Mr. Lee	Well, you know what they say, "No news is good news."
Doug	Hey, Ricky, how would you like to do your favorite brother a big favor? Could you and some of your friends give me a hand packing on Saturday?
Ricky	Sure, I guess so.
Doug	Thanks, Ricky. You're a great brother.

2. Listen in

Meanwhile in Chicago, Carlos, one of Laura's coworkers, gives her a telephone message. Read the statements below. Then listen to the conversation and choose *a* or *b*.

1. Chuck wants Laura _____ .
   a. to call him back
   b. to meet him after work

2. Laura is expecting Jack Thomson _____ .
   a. to call her
   b. to come to the office

3

(*Laura dials Chuck's number.*)

Chuck	Hello?
Laura	Hi, Chuck. You sound kind of depressed. Is anything wrong?
Chuck	Remember I was starting to worry when I hadn't heard anything in two weeks? Well, today I got a call. . . .

4. Figure it out

Say *True, False,* or *It doesn't say.*

1. Doug didn't get the new job.
2. Doug has already found an apartment in Chicago.
3. Doug is expecting someone at his apartment.
4. Ricky and his friends are going to help Doug.
5. Doug and Chuck probably applied for the same job.

44. Your turn

Work with a partner. Look at the pictures and try to figure out what each person's job is. Describe what each person has to do on a typical work day.

Discuss these questions in groups.

1. Of these six jobs, which one is the most interesting to you? The least interesting? Why?
2. Do you have a job? If so, describe what you do on a typical work day.

Here are some things people think about when they are looking for a job. In groups, discuss which of these would be most important to you. Can you add to the list?

- good salary and benefits
- independence: being your own boss
- physical activity

- excitement
- variety: doing many different things

- working with people
- travel
- working outdoors

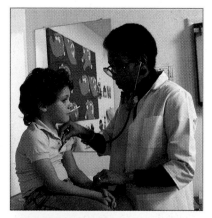

How to say it

Practice the phrases. Then practice the conversation.

call her	[kɔ́lər]	ask him	[ǽskɪm]
called him	[kɔ́ldɪm]	tell him	[tɛlɪ́m]

A Bill is back from lunch.
B Anne Murphy called him before. Tell him to call her back right away. And ask him to call Beth Watson too.

45.

KNOW WHAT YOU'RE WORTH BEFORE YOU SEEK A RAISE

Look at exercise 3 at the bottom of the page and write your answer to the last question: "What will you say?" After you've read the article, look at your answer again and see if you would change it in any way.

by Cynthia Hanson

Do you think you deserve a raise? Then ask for it.

In today's corporate climate, most regular salary hikes have shrunk or disappeared. Increasingly, employment experts say you'll have to ask if you want a pay boost.

"If you won't fight for what you're worth, what you're saying is 'I don't know if I have similar market value elsewhere,'" says Marilyn Moats Kennedy, a career counselor in Wilmette, Illinois.

Further, says John Leonard, a New York career management consultant, it's part of your job to make your case: "For you to get a raise, management has to think you're valuable. And no one will really know your brilliance unless you tell them."

Fearing that they'll be denied a raise, many people never request one. But experts say you'll gain respect if you make a strong case and deliver it in a professional manner.

How can you increase your chances? Experts offer these strategies:

• Do your homework. "You must know the industry standard for your job and where you fall on the salary scale at your company," Leonard says. Professional associations and coworkers are excellent sources.

• Think timing. If your boss submits annual budgets in September, request an appointment in July. Or take advantage of the success of an important assignment by seeking a raise after you've made a significant contribution.

• Quantify your accomplishments. To get a raise,

you'll have to demonstrate how your performance contributes to the company's profits.

• Keep it career-focused. Whining about your salary will kill your chances for a raise. Steer the discussion to your contributions over the past year and your desire for career growth. And never threaten to quit. "When people say, 'Give me more money or I'll leave,' more often than not, the boss says, 'I wish you good luck,'" Leonard says.

• Rehearse. "You must come across as serious and prepared, not casual," Kennedy says. It's helpful to outline your achievements on paper, then practice delivering them aloud, either in front of a mirror, before a friend, or on a video.

• Know what you want. It's crucial to specify either a percentage increase or salary figure that should be in line with your market value and accomplishments. If you're turned down for an increase, ask for a reason and another review in six months. As a last resort, ask for alternatives such as more vacation time or the opportunity to attend training seminars. Both are likely to be easier to negotiate than a bigger paycheck.

• Follow-up. Regardless of the outcome, thank your boss for the meeting, either in a personal note or computer message. A healthy relationship with your boss is essential to your career growth and courtesy will keep it on track.

---

1. **Match the words from the article with the best meanings.**

1. seek	a. saying
2. boost	b. complaining
3. denied	c. appear to be
4. whining	d. measure
5. steer	e. final try
6. quantify	f. working smoothly
7. come across as	g. raise
8. delivering	h. turned down for
9. last resort	i. ask for
10. on track	j. direct

2. **What does "Do your homework" mean in this article? What is meant by the expression "I wish you good luck"?**

3. **Have you ever asked for a pay raise? Did you get it? Why or why not? Imagine you are going to ask for a pay raise. What will you say?**

PREVIEW

FUNCTIONS/THEMES	LANGUAGE	FORMS
Talk about exercise Talk about likes and dislikes	Do you ever get any exercise? Do you like to swim? I ought to exercise more, but I can never seem to find the time. I've always enjoyed swimming. I hate getting up early on weekends.	Infinitives vs. gerunds
Talk about weight and height	Has he lost (a lot of) weight? Yeah. Twenty pounds. How tall is he? Five foot ten.	
Invite someone	I'm going biking with Bill and a friend of ours on Saturday. How about joining us?	Possessive pronouns and possessives of names
Ask where to get something	Do you know where I can rent a bike?	
Talk about your family	She's a lot like me. She's very different from me. Did you use to get along when you were younger? Not too well. We used to fight a lot.	The past with *used to*

Preview the conversations.

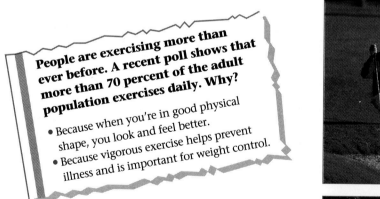

People are exercising more than ever before. A recent poll shows that more than 70 percent of the adult population exercises daily. Why?

- Because when you're in good physical shape, you look and feel better.
- Because vigorous exercise helps prevent illness and is important for weight control.

1. Read the article about exercise. Then choose a partner and discuss these questions.

   a. How often do you exercise? What kinds of exercise do you like?
   b. What kinds of exercise are popular in your country?

2. Work with other classmates. Talk about a sport or exercise you've always wanted to learn.

46. You're in great shape!

Karen and Dennis run into a friend while they're taking a walk.

A

Mike Hi, Dennis! Hi, Karen!

Dennis Mike! Hey, you've lost a lot of weight.

Mike Forty pounds.

Dennis No kidding! How much do you weigh now?

Mike Around 160 pounds.

Karen You're in great shape, Mike.

Mike Well, I get a lot of exercise.

Dennis I really ought to start doing something. I'm starting to get a potbelly.

B

Mike Do you ever get any exercise, Dennis?

Dennis Not regularly. I've always hated running.

Mike Well, why don't you do something else?

Dennis I enjoy biking. In fact, I used to go on long bike trips, but lately I can never seem to find the time.

Mike Well, here's your big chance. I'm biking to Lake Walden next weekend with some friends of mine. How about joining us, both of you?

Karen Sounds great!

Dennis Well, I was planning to work Saturday. . . .

Karen Oh, come on, Dennis. You can work some other time. Uh, do you know where I can rent a bike, Mike?

Mike There's a bicycle shop somewhere around here. Say, how tall are you?

Karen Five four.

Mike You're about the same height as my sister . . . or maybe an inch taller. She has two bikes. I'm sure you can borrow one of hers.

Figure it out

1. Listen to the conversations. Then choose *a* or *b*.

1. a. Dennis probably hasn't seen Mike for a long time.
   b. Dennis probably sees Mike every week.
2. a. Dennis wants to start running, but can't find the time.
   b. Dennis doesn't get enough exercise.

2. Listen again and say *True, False,* or *It doesn't say.*

1. Mike used to weigh 200 pounds.
2. Dennis used to exercise more.
3. Dennis likes to run.
4. Dennis has been too busy to take long bike trips.
5. Karen doesn't have her own bike.
6. Mike's sister is going to Lake Walden next weekend too.
7. Mike's sister is a year older than he is.
8. Mike and his sister used to fight a lot.

3. Fill in the blanks with *to work* or *working.*

1. I enjoy *working*.
2. I was planning _____ .
3. I'm _____ tomorrow.
4. I used _____ harder.
5. How about _____ late?

C

Dennis I didn't know you had a sister, Mike.
Mike I have a twin sister.
Dennis Really? Is she just like you?
Mike Oh no. She's very different from me. To tell the truth, we don't really have much in common, but we get along really well.
Dennis Did you use to get along when you were younger?
Mike Oh, yeah. We've always gotten along well.
Dennis You're lucky. My brother and I used to fight all the time.

47. I've always enjoyed swimming.

1 ▶ Listen to the conversation. Circle *W* for the things the woman likes to do in her free time. Circle *M* for the things the man likes to do.

W M	W M	W M	W M
1. play tennis	2. run	3. roller-skate	4. ice-skate

2 ▶ Listen to the two possible conversations.
▶ Act out similar conversations with a partner. Use the activities in the pictures above or your own information.

A Do you like to swim?

B Yes, I've always enjoyed swimming. In fact, I've started swimming regularly.

B No, I've never liked swimming very much.

> I've always liked swimming.
> I've always enjoyed swimming.
> I've never liked swimming.
> I've always hated swimming.

3 ▶ Study the frames: Infinitives vs. gerunds

I love I like I hate I've started	**to swim.** **swimming.**
I enjoy I've stopped	**swimming.**

Gerunds, such as *swimming*, are formed the same way as present participles, by adding -*ing*.

4 ▶ Listen to the conversation.
▶ In groups of three, have similar conversations using the pictures below or your own information.

A I like to get up early on weekends.
B Me too. I like to get up early and enjoy the whole day.
C Not me! I hate getting up early on weekends.

I like to paint.	I like to play soccer.	I like to read.	I like to sleep late.

5 ▶ Talk to your classmates. Find out what they like to do on the weekend. Find out what they hate to do. Report to the class.

Yong Hee and Carlos both like shopping.
Lee hates to clean the house.

6 ► **Listen to the conversation and practice it with a partner.**
► **Act out similar conversations, using your own information.**

A Do you ever get any exercise?
B I run five miles a day. How about you?
A Hardly ever. I ought to exercise more, but I can never seem to find the time.

ought to = should

Do you ever get any exercise?
I run five miles a day.
I play tennis every other day.
I work out three times a week.
Sometimes I roller-skate.
I go biking once in a while.
I used to swim, but I haven't lately.
Hardly ever.
I can never seem to find the time.

TALK ABOUT WEIGHT AND HEIGHT

7 ► **Match the descriptions with the pictures.**
► **How much does each person weigh now?**

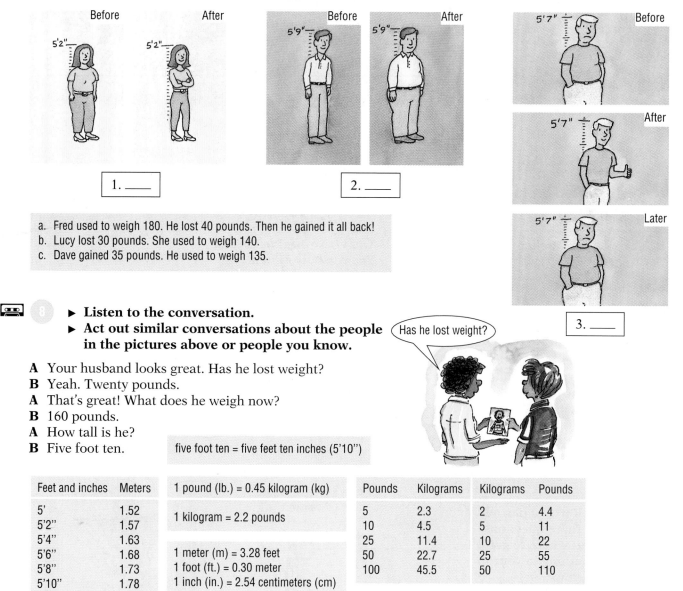

Before   After   Before   After   Before

5'2"   5'2"   5'9"   5'9"   5'7"

1. ____   2. ____   After   5'7"   Later   5'7"

a. Fred used to weigh 180. He lost 40 pounds. Then he gained it all back!
b. Lucy lost 30 pounds. She used to weigh 140.
c. Dave gained 35 pounds. He used to weigh 135.

3. ____

8 ► **Listen to the conversation.**
► **Act out similar conversations about the people in the pictures above or people you know.**

Has he lost weight?

A Your husband looks great. Has he lost weight?
B Yeah. Twenty pounds.
A That's great! What does he weigh now?
B 160 pounds.
A How tall is he?
B Five foot ten.

five foot ten = five feet ten inches (5'10")

Feet and inches	Meters
5'	1.52
5'2"	1.57
5'4"	1.63
5'6"	1.68
5'8"	1.73
5'10"	1.78
6'	1.83

1 pound (lb.) = 0.45 kilogram (kg)

1 kilogram = 2.2 pounds

1 meter (m) = 3.28 feet
1 foot (ft.) = 0.30 meter
1 inch (in.) = 2.54 centimeters (cm)

Pounds	Kilograms	Kilograms	Pounds
5	2.3	2	4.4
10	4.5	5	11
25	11.4	10	22
50	22.7	25	55
100	45.5	50	110

For more weights and measures, see p. 86.

48. I'm going biking with a friend of mine.

1
▶ Listen to the two possible conversations and practice them with a partner.
▶ Act out similar conversations, using the activities in the pictures or your own information.

A I'm going biking with Bill and a friend of ours on Saturday. How about joining us?

B Sounds great.   **B** Well, I was planning to work on Saturday.

> **Other ways to say it**
>
> Would you like to join us?
> Do you want to come along?
> Why don't you come with us?

2
▶ Study the frame: Possessive pronouns and possessives of names

a friend	of	mine
		yours
		his
		hers
		ours
		theirs
		John's

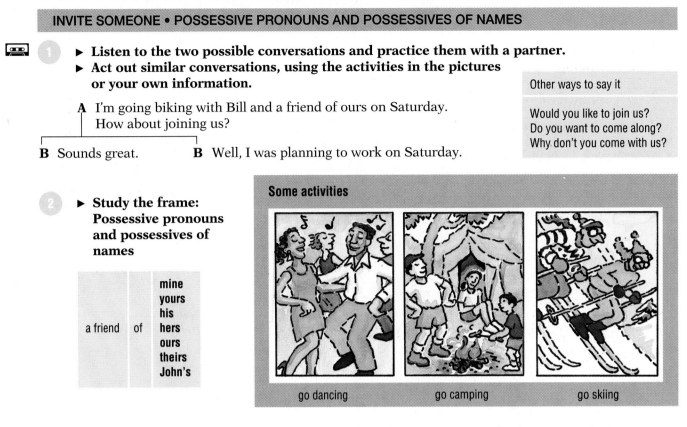

Some activities

go dancing   go camping   go skiing

3
▶ Listen to the two possible conversations and practice them with a partner.

A Do you know where I can rent a bike?

B There's a bicycle shop on Main Street. It's called Hot Wheels.   **B** Oh, I have one I never use. You can borrow mine.

> rent a car
> buy a newspaper
> get a good haircut
> make a phone call

4
▶ Complete the conversations with questions, using the phrases in the box.
▶ Listen to check your work.
▶ Practice the conversations with a partner.

1. ____? — Yeah, at the newsstand down the street.

2. ____? — Sure. There's a public phone over there.

5
▶ Work with a partner. Ask three questions about where to get something in your city, town, or neighborhood. Your partner will answer.

3. ____? — I know a great hairstylist, but he's expensive.

4. ____? — There's a car rental place about a mile from here.

49. Is your sister like you?

1
- ▶ **Listen to the two possible conversations and practice them with a partner.**
- ▶ **Act out similar conversations, using your own information.**

A Is your sister older than you or younger?
B She's five years older.
A Do you have a lot in common?

B Yes. We're a lot alike. We both enjoy doing things outdoors.
B Not really. Our interests are very different. (She likes . . .)

Is your sister like you? Do you have a lot in common?	She's a lot like me. We're very similar. She's very different from me.	She's five years older. We're twins. She's two years younger.

2
- ▶ **Interview two classmates about their families. Report to the class.**

Marie has an older brother. Their interests are very different.
She likes . . . but her brother enjoys . . .

3
- ▶ **Listen to the two possible conversations and practice them with a partner.**
- ▶ **Act out similar conversations, using your own information.**

A Do you get along with your sister?
B Yes. Most of the time.
A Did you use to get along when you were younger?

B Yes. We've always gotten along well.
B Not too well. We used to fight a lot.

> Use *used to* to refer to something that took place repeatedly or over an extended period of time in the past:
>
> I **used to** take the bus to work.
> I **used to** live in Mexico.

4
- ▶ **Study the frames: The past with *used to***

Where	**did** you		work?			**used to**	take the bus to work.
	Did you	**use to**	drive	to work?	I	**didn't use to**	drive to work, but I do now.
						never **used to**	drive to work, but I do now.

5
- ▶ **Amy started a new job a few months ago. Complete her conversation with Jim. Use a form of *used to* and the verb in parentheses in each answer.**
- ▶ **Listen to check your work.**

Jim <u>What did you use to do</u> (do) before you came here?
Amy I was marketing director at Lowell and White.
Jim Oh, then you _____ (work) with Don Ford.
Amy Yes. As a matter of fact, we're good friends.
Jim _____ (travel) a lot for that job too?
Amy Hardly ever. That's something I love about this job. Of course I work harder now. I never _____ (work) late at the office on my old job.

50. A little exercise will do you good.

Doug is moving out of his apartment.

1

Ricky	Hey, what did you put in this box? It weighs a ton.
Doug	Oh, stop complaining. A little exercise will do you good.
Ricky	I get plenty of exercise already. I play basketball every day. In fact, I was planning to play today.
Doug	Well, we're almost finished. I guess I have more stuff than I thought. How about working, say, fifteen minutes more? Then we can order out for pizza. I'll treat.
Ricky	Sounds great. I'm so hungry I could eat a horse.
Sarah	Where do you want me to put this, Doug?
Doug	Hey, isn't that too heavy for you, Sarah?
Sarah	This is nothing. I lift weights.
Doug	Well, here, let me help you anyway. (*Grunts*) This box is heavier than I thought.
Ricky	I guess a little exercise would do you good. Maybe you ought to lift weights like Sarah.
Doug	Maybe I should. I used to be a lot stronger.
Sarah	You mean when you were young?
Doug	Funny, I thought I still was.

2. Figure it out

Say *True, False,* or *It doesn't say.*

1. Ricky hardly ever gets any exercise.
2. Doug, Ricky, and Sarah started working more than an hour ago.
3. Doug, Ricky, and Sarah are going to order a pizza in fifteen minutes.
4. Doug is going to pay for the pizza.
5. Doug isn't as strong as he was when he was younger.

3. Listen in

Sarah and Doug continue their conversation. Read the questions below. Then listen to the conversation and answer the questions.

1. Who is Ruth?
2. How tall is Ruth?
3. What has Ruth always enjoyed doing?

51. Your turn

Fill out the questionnaire and find out how long you will live.

If you received a low score, remember that it's never too late to change. What changes do you think you should make in your life? Discuss your answers with a partner.

How Long Will You Live?

We don't know how long we will live, but we do know that certain factors can lengthen or shorten a person's life. Use the questionnaire below to calculate (approximately) how many years you will live.

START WITH THE NUMBER 75.   75

1. SEX:

If you are a man,	subtract 3	____
If you are a woman,	add 4	____

2. LIFESTYLE:

If you live in a big city (over 2 million),	-3	____
If you live in a small town (under 10,000),	+2	____
If you work at a desk,	-3	____
If your work requires physical activity,	+3	____
If you exercise a lot (5 times a week for 30 minutes),	+2	____
If you live with someone,	+5	____
If you live alone,	-1	____

3. PERSONALITY:

If you sleep more than 10 hours a night,	-4	____
If you sleep less than 5 hours a night,	-4	____
If you are impatient,	-3	____
If you are easygoing,	+3	____
If you are happy,	+1	____
If you are unhappy,	-2	____

4. SUCCESS:

If you earn over $50,000 a year,	-2	____
If you finished college,	+1	____
If you have more than one college degree,	+2	____
If you are 65 years old and still working,	+3	____

5. FAMILY BACKGROUND:

If any of your grandparents lived to 85,	+2	____
If all four of your grandparents lived to 80,	+6	____
If either of your parents died of a heart attack before 50,	-4	____
If any parent, brother, or sister has heart disease or diabetes,	-3	____

6. HEALTH:

If you smoke more than 2 packs of cigarettes a day,	-8	____
If you smoke more than half a pack of cigarettes a day,	-3	____
If you are overweight by 50 pounds,	-8	____
30 pounds,	-3	____
15 pounds,	-2	____
If you have a medical exam every year,	+2	____

7. AGE ADJUSTMENT:

If you are 30-40,	+2	____
40-50,	+3	____
50-70,	+4	____
If you are over 70,	+5	____

YOU WILL LIVE APPROXIMATELY_____YEARS.

How to say it

**Practice the phrases.
Then practice the conversation.**

some friends of Bill's
                [z]

a cousin of Lois's
                [ɪz]

a friend of Pat's
                [s]

A I'm going skiing with Pat and some friends of Bill's on Saturday. One of them is a cousin of Lois's.

B Really? A friend of Pat's called me last night and invited me too. But I don't ski.

An Exercise Program for the Traveler

Have you ever taken a long flight? Do you ever exercise in your seat when you fly? Look at the pictures in the article. Do you think these exercises would be helpful on a long flight?

The human body is made to move and it works best when it gets regular exercise. These days, however, we spend a lot of time sitting down—in an office chair, at the theater, or in a comfortable airline seat—where there is very little freedom of movement. Here is an exercise program that will help keep you comfortable on long trips so that you arrive refreshed and relaxed.

1. Jogging on the spot.
A warm-up exercise.
Lift your heels as high as possible, one foot at a time. At the same time, lift your arms in a bent position and move forward and backward as if you were walking. Continue for 1–3 minutes.

2. Shoulder rolling.
For shoulder joints and muscles.
Move your shoulders gently in large circles in both forward and backward directions. Repeat 6 times in each direction.

3. Forward bending with stomach in.
For your stomach muscles.
Pull in your stomach. Bend forward while lifting your toes high. Put your toes back on the floor, relax your stomach, and sit up again. Repeat 30 times.

4. Head turning and nodding.
For your neck and spine.
Turn your head all the way to the right. Nod a few times. Do the same to the left. Repeat 6 times on each side.

5. Hand turning.
For your wrists.
Turn your hands over and open your fingers. Return your hands to their first position and relax them. Repeat 15 times.

6. Knees and elbows.
For blood circulation.
Raise your right knee to your left elbow. Then raise your left knee to your right elbow. Repeat 10 times.

1. Read the article. Then match the parts of the body with the words below.

a. heel
b. elbow
c. neck
d. toes
e. fingers
f. stomach
g. shoulder
h. head
i. hand
j. foot
k. arm
l. knee

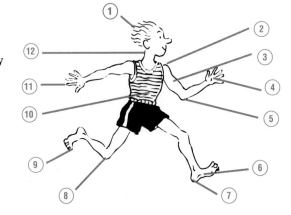

2. Practice doing each exercise.

1. Which exercise is the easiest for you?
2. Which exercise is the hardest for you?

Review of units 5-7

1. ▶ Use the map to figure out a question to complete each conversation. Then combine each pair of sentences in brackets [ ], using *when*, *until*, or *as soon as*.

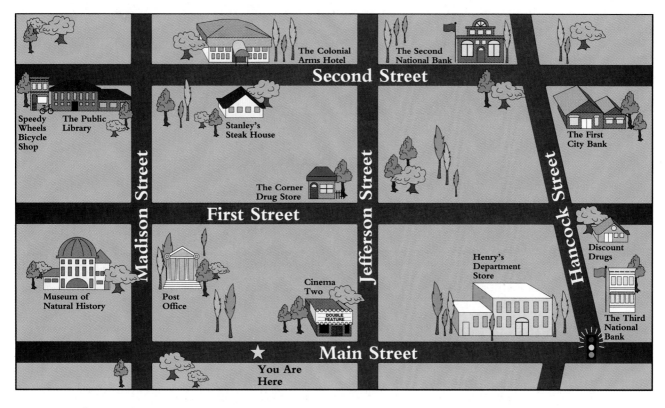

1. **A** *How do I get to Discount Drugs?*
   B Go straight ahead on Main.
   [You'll pass a big department store. Turn left.]
   as soon as
   As soon as you pass a big department store, *turn left.*
   It'll be on your right near the end of the block.

2. **A** _____?
   B It's on Madison Street.
   [Go to the corner. Then turn right.] *when*
   That's Madison.
   [Then go straight ahead. You'll come to a post office.] *until*
   It's right across the street from the post office.

3. **A** _____?
   B There's one about three blocks from here.
   [Walk to the corner. Then turn left on Jefferson.] *when*
   [Stay on Jefferson. You'll get to Second Street.] *until*
   Turn left. It'll be on your right, about halfway down the block.

4. **A** _____?
   B Yes, it's the next street after Jefferson.
   [Just stay on Main. You'll come to a traffic light.] *until*
   There'll be a big department store on your left. You can't miss it.

2A ▶ **Student A follows the instructions below. Student B follows the instuctions on page 78.**

Student A You're walking along the street in front of Henry's Department Store. Student B stops you on the street and asks for information. Use the map to answer Student B's questions.

2B ▸ **Student B follows the instructions below. Student A follows the instuctions on page 77.**

Student B You're riding your bike and you get a flat tire right in front of Henry's Department Store. Stop Student A on the street and ask where you can get your tired fixed. When Student A recommends a place, ask how to get there.

3 ▸ **This woman is looking for a shoe repair shop. Read the statements below. Listen to the conversation and then say *True* or *False*.**

1. Ed's Shoe Repair is closer than Tony's.
2. Ed's is fifteen minutes away by bus.

4 ▸ **This man is asking for information. Complete the conversation with the comparative or superlative form of the adjectives in parentheses.**
▸ **Listen to check your work.**

A I'm looking for a place to stay. Could you recommend a good hotel?

B Well, The Colonial Arms is _the nicest_ (nice) hotel in town, but it's also _____ (expensive). Rooms start at $200 a night.

A Oh! Is there anything _____ (expensive)?

B Let me see. The Windsor is a lot _____ (reasonable), but it's _____ (far) away. You'll have to take a taxi to get there.

A O.K., but I need to get some cash. Is there a bank with a 24-hour cash machine near here?

B Actually, there are three—the Third National, the Second National, and the First City.

A Which one is _____ (easy) to get to?

B Well, the Third National is _____ (close) than the other two. It's only about two blocks from here.

A Thank you. You've been very helpful.

B You're welcome.

5

▶ Nick calls his friend Wendy at her office and leaves a message for her. Put the conversation in order.

▶ Listen to check your work.

___ I'll give her the message as soon as she gets back.

___ Yes, please. This is Nick Damato. Would you please ask her to call me? My number is 555-3929.

___ She should be back by two. Would you like to leave a message?

___ Can I speak to Wendy Jacobs, please?

___ When do you expect her back?

_1_ Good afternoon, Rockwell and Stone.

___ Thank you.

___ I'm sorry, but she's not in the office right now.

6

▶ **Work with a partner. Play these roles.**

Student A Call a friend's office and ask the receptionist (Student B) if you can speak to your friend. If your friend is not there, leave a message.

Student B Play the role of the receptionist. Student A calls and wants to speak to someone who's not in the office now. Offer to take a message. Complete the message form.

For _____
Date _____
                                      Time _____
M _____   WHILE YOU WERE OUT
From _____
Phone No. _____
☐ TELEPHONED
☐ PLEASE CALL
☐ WILL CALL AGAIN
☐ RETURNED YOUR CALL   ☐ URGENT
                              ☐ WANTS TO SEE YOU
                              ☐ CAME TO SEE YOU
Message _____
_____
_____
_____

7

▶ **Listen to the first part of each conversation and choose the best response.**

1. a. Well, the most expensive one I can think of is Alfredo's.
   b. Well, the closest one I can think of is Alfredo's.

2. a. No, I'm afraid I don't.
   b. No, that place is too far.

3. a. It's faster by bus.
   b. It's about a ten-minute walk.

4. a. Oh, I'll get one for you.
   b. I'd be glad to.

5. a. May I tell him who's calling?
   b. I'll give him the message.

6. a. Oh, I'll copy them for you.
   b. Oh, I'll copy it for you.

7. a. Me too. I enjoy getting up early.
   b. Not me. I like to get up early.

8. a. Sure. There's a coffee shop just down the street.
   b. Sure. There's one on Main Street.

9. a. O.K. Sounds like fun.
   b. O.K. I've never liked dancing.

10. a. No, I can't seem to find the time.
    b. Yes, I used to play tennis.

8 ▶ **Martha White just celebrated her one hundredth birthday. Read the interview about her life and about "the old days."**

MARTHA WHITE:
Clinton's Oldest Citizen

Mrs. White, have you always lived in Clinton?

All my life. As a matter of fact, I was born in this house. That's the way it used to be in the old days. People never used to move away from their home town. You were born in a place, and you lived there until you died.

Your first husband died ten years ago...

Yes, at the age of ninety-two. We had seventy wonderful years together. We were very much alike. Both of us loved a good conversation. People used to talk to each other more in the old days. Now they watch television.

Mrs. White, you've already lived a hundred years and you look as if you might live another hundred years. What's your secret?

Well, I laugh a lot. That's very important.

And I keep busy. I get a lot of exercise too. I've always enjoyed sports. I went skiing and horseback riding regularly until I was eighty-five. And I've always liked swimming. In fact, I still swim every day at the high school pool, and I've started running a little with my second husband.

When did you remarry?

Six years ago. I was ninety-four and he was a young man of eighty. A lot of people say I robbed the cradle!

Mrs. White, you're a hundred years old now. How do you feel?

Great! Not a day over ninety!

▶ **Talk about two things that used to be different in the old days, according to Mrs. White.**

9 ▶ **How have things changed since you, your parents, or your grandparents were children? Make statements with *used to*, *didn't use to*, *never used to*, and *not ... anymore.***

People didn't use to work on computers.
People used to use manual typewriters.

10 ▶ **Work with a partner. Compare yourself to a family member. Are you alike or different? Be as specific as you can.**

I'm a lot like my father. We both like... We both enjoy...

11 ▶ **Imagine you're celebrating your one hundredth birthday. Write a short article about yourself, telling about the things you've always liked to do, things you've never enjoyed doing, things you used to do, and things you never used to do. Before starting to write, follow the steps below.**

1. Make a list of things you've always liked to do.
2. Make a list of things you've never enjoyed doing.
3. Make a list of things you used to do, but don't do anymore.
4. Make a list of things that you never used to do, but that you've started doing.

PREVIEW

FUNCTIONS/THEMES	LANGUAGE	FORMS
Apologize for calling at a bad time	I hope I didn't wake you up. I'm sorry to call so late. I was (just) watching TV.	The past continuous
Ask if someone has plans Invite someone	Are you doing anything on Saturday? How about coming over (for dinner) on Saturday? What time do you want us to come? I hope (that) you can make it. I don't think (that) I'm busy. But let me check my calendar.	*Hope* and *think*
Check plans with someone Talk about plans	We have theater tickets for Saturday, don't we? He'd like us to come over later.	Tag questions Infinitives after object pronouns
Refresh your memory Identify someone	What does he do again? He's the one who just got married.	

Preview the conversations.

Read the letter. Then continue the conversation between the two roommates.

> Dear _____
> So much has happened since the last time we saw each other. The big news is that I just got married to Patricia Chen. She's a geologist. I met her here in Texas. I've been here for two years now, doing graduate work in archeology. I'd really like you to meet Patricia. We'll be in town the week of July 2, and we'll be staying with my parents. I hope we can get together then. I'll give you a call when I get to town. I hope all is well with you.
>
> See you soon!
>
> Ed

I just got a letter from Ed Riley.

Who's Ed Riley?

Roommate 1
You just received this letter from Ed Riley, an old friend from college. Tell your roommate who Ed is and what his plans are.

Roommate 2
Your roommate tells you about a letter from Ed Riley. Act interested and ask a lot of questions. Find out who Ed is and what he said.

53. Let me check with In Sook.

Nancy gets a phone call from Ed Riley.

A

(Telephone rings)

Nancy Hello?

Ed Hello, Nancy? This is Ed Riley.

Nancy Ed! How are you? Congratulations!

Ed Thanks. I'm sorry to call so late. I hope I didn't wake you up.

Nancy Oh, no. I was just watching TV.

Ed Listen, are you doing anything on Saturday evening?

Nancy I don't think I am.

Ed Then how about coming over for dinner? Bring your roommate too.

Nancy I'd love to, but let me check with In Sook before I tell you for sure. She wasn't feeling well, so she went to bed early.

Ed I hope it's nothing serious.

Nancy No, I think it's just a cold. What time do you want us to come?

Ed Oh, about seven. You've been to my parents' house, haven't you?

Nancy Yes, but it's been a while. What's their address again?

Ed It's 3820 Warren Street. It's off Wisconsin Avenue.

Nancy Oh, yes, I think I remember now. Well, let's say tentatively that we're coming, and I'll let you know if we can't make it.

Ed I really hope you can come.

Nancy I do too. I haven't seen you for so long.

Ed So . . . tell me what's happening in *your* life. . . .

Nancy I got a call from Ed Riley last night.
In Sook Who's that?
Nancy Don't you remember? He's the one who just got married.
In Sook Oh, right, the archeologist. What does his wife do again?
Nancy She's a geologist. Anyway, they'd like us to go to his parents' house for dinner Saturday.
In Sook We have theater tickets for Saturday, don't we? We're going with Mike and Chris.
Nancy Oh, I completely forgot! I'd better call him back right now.

Figure it out

1. Listen to the conversations and choose the correct answers.

1. a. Nancy and Ed have spoken to each other recently.
   b. Nancy and Ed haven't spoken to each other since Ed got married.

2. a. Nancy and In Sook are going to see a play on Saturday.
   b. Nancy and In Sook haven't made plans for Saturday.

2. Listen again and say *True, False,* or *It doesn't say.*

1. Nancy was awakened when Ed called.   *False.*
2. Nancy didn't think she and In Sook were busy on Saturday.
3. Ed has been married to a geologist for a few years.
4. In Sook gets colds often.
5. Nancy goes to Ed's parents' house often.

3. Choose *a* or *b*.

1. I hope it's
   a. nothing serious.
   b. anything serious.

2. I don't think I'm doing
   a. something.
   b. anything.

3. You've been there,
   a. haven't you?
   b. don't you?

4. What time do you want
   a. us to come.
   b. we come.

54. I hope I didn't wake you up.

1 ▶ Listen to the conversations. What were these people doing when the phone rang?

1. *He was watching TV.*   2. _____   3. _____   4. _____

2 ▶ Listen to the telephone conversation.
▶ Act out similar conversations with a partner. Use your own names and the information in the boxes.

A Hello?
B Hello, Matt? This is Judy. I hope I didn't wake you up.
A Oh, no. I was just watching TV.

Some questions
Did I wake you up?
Did I get you out of bed?
Am I calling at a bad time?
Am I interrupting your dinner?

What you were doing when the phone rang	
watching TV	getting ready for work
making breakfast	listening to the radio
reading the paper	doing some homework
doing the dishes	studying for a test

3 ▶ Complete each conversation with an apology from the box.
▶ Listen to check your work.

I'm sorry to call . . .	so late.
	so early.
	at dinner time.

1. **A** *I'm sorry to call so late.*
   B Oh, that's O.K. I'm still up.

2. **A** _____
   B Oh, that's O.K. We haven't started eating yet.

3. **A** _____
   B No problem. I've been up for hours.

4. **A** _____
   B It *is* kind of late. I've been in bed since ten.

55. Are you doing anything on Saturday?

1

▶ **Listen to the two possible conversations.**

▶ **Act out similar conversations with a partner, using the information in the calendar.**

A Are you doing anything on Saturday?

B I don't think I am. But let me check my calendar. . . .

B No, I'm not doing anything on Saturday.

B I'm sorry. I already have plans for Saturday.

Other ways to say it
I don't think I'm busy.
I don't think so.
I think I'm busy.
I think I am.

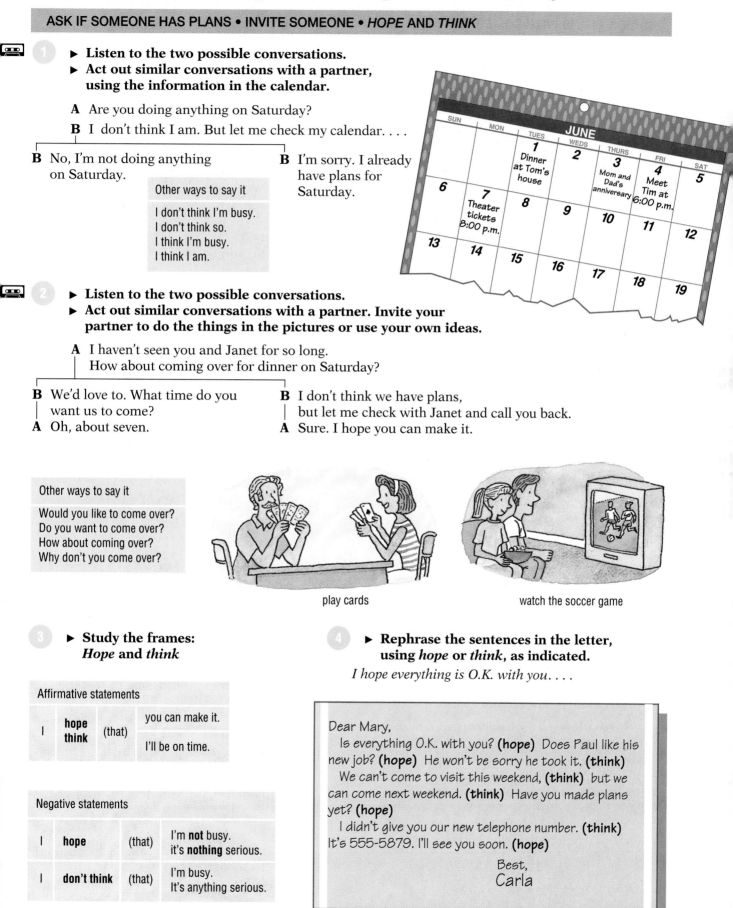

JUNE

SUN	MON	TUES	WEDS	THURS	FRI	SAT
		1 Dinner at Tom's house	2	3 Mom and Dad's anniversary	4 Meet Tim at 6:00 p.m.	5
6	7 Theater tickets 8:00 p.m.	8	9	10	11	12
13	14	15	16	17	18	19

2

▶ **Listen to the two possible conversations.**

▶ **Act out similar conversations with a partner. Invite your partner to do the things in the pictures or use your own ideas.**

A I haven't seen you and Janet for so long.
How about coming over for dinner on Saturday?

B We'd love to. What time do you want us to come?

A Oh, about seven.

B I don't think we have plans, but let me check with Janet and call you back.

A Sure. I hope you can make it.

Other ways to say it
Would you like to come over?
Do you want to come over?
How about coming over?
Why don't you come over?

play cards

watch the soccer game

3

▶ **Study the frames:**
Hope and *think*

4

▶ **Rephrase the sentences in the letter, using *hope* or *think*, as indicated.**

I hope everything is O.K. with you. . . .

Affirmative statements

| I | **hope**
think | (that) | you can make it. |
| | | | I'll be on time. |

Negative statements

I	**hope**	(that)	I'm **not** busy.
			it's **nothing** serious.
I	**don't think**	(that)	I'm busy.
			It's anything serious.

Dear Mary,

Is everything O.K. with you? **(hope)** Does Paul like his new job? **(hope)** He won't be sorry he took it. **(think)**

We can't come to visit this weekend, **(think)** but we can come next weekend. **(think)** Have you made plans yet? **(hope)**

I didn't give you our new telephone number. **(think)** It's 555-5879. I'll see you soon. **(hope)**

Best,
Carla

5 ▶ **Two people are discussing their plans for the long holiday weekend.**
Listen and fill in their calendar with things they're planning to do.

Friday December 30	**Saturday** December 31 New Year's Eve	**Sunday** January 1 New Year's Day	**Monday** January 2
○ _____ _____ _____ ○ _____	○ _____ _____ _____ ○ _____	○ _____ _____ _____ ○ _____	○ _____ _____ _____ ○ _____

6 ▶ **Listen to the conversation and practice it with a partner.**
▶ **Act out similar conversations, using the names of people you know and invitations for the activities in the pictures below.**

A Ed Riley called last night. He'd like us to come over on Saturday.
B But we have theater tickets for Saturday, don't we?
A Oh, I completely forgot! I'd better call him back right now.

SOME ACTIVITIES

go to a barbecue on Sunday

come over for lunch tomorrow

play golf on Saturday morning

go to a nightclub on Friday night

7 ▶ **Study the frame: Tag questions**

You usually say tag questions with rising intonation when you are asking questions and are not sure that the other person will agree. You usually say tag questions with falling intonation when you are asking questions and are almost sure the other person will agree.

We have theater tickets for Saturday, **don't we**?
We're going to a concert, **aren't we**?
Diana wants us to come over, **doesn't she**?
Sam invited us to go to the movies, **didn't he**?
Jenny is working late, **isn't she**?
You have to pick up your passport, **don't you**?

Tag questions, such as *don't we?*, are often used to confirm or clarify information.

8 ▶ **Two roommates are talking. Complete the conversation with tag questions.**
▶ **Listen to check your work.**

A We have plans for Friday night, _____ ?
B That's right. We're going to a party at Dave and Sally's.
A Oh, yeah. I forgot! It's at eight o'clock, _____ ?
B No, it's late, at ten. You can still come, _____ ?
A Sure, I can. Joe will be there, _____ ? I haven't seen him for a long time.
B Yeah, and he's bringing his cousin, Sandy. You know her, _____ ?
A Yeah, I do. She's really nice, _____ ?
B I don't know. I've never met her.

9

Study the frame:
Infinitives after object
pronouns

He	'd like invited asked wants	me you him her us them	**to come** over. **to go** to the movies.

10 ▶ **Complete each conversation, using the verbs in parentheses. There may be several possible answers.**

1. **A** Who were you just talking to?
   B That was Jane.
   I asked her to come over (come over) later.

2. **A** Hi. Did anyone call?
   B Harry did. He _____
   (have) dinner at his house.

3. **A** Are you busy tomorrow morning?
   B I think I am. Marie _____
   (go) shopping with her.

4. **A** How was your day?
   B Fine. I ran into Jane and Ted on my way
   home. I _____ (play)
   tennis with us tomorrow.

5. **A** I'm back. Any messages?
   B Yes. Neil called right after you left. He
   _____ (help) him with his
   French homework.

11 ▶ **Listen to the conversation.**
▶ **Imagine you know the people in the pictures. Act out similar conversations with a partner.**
▶ **Work with the same partner. Have similar conversations about people you both know.**

A I got a phone call from Ed Riley.
B Who's that?
A Don't you remember? He's the one who just got married.
B Oh, yeah. What does he do again?
A He's an archeologist.

You got a phone call from Ed Riley. He just got married. He's an archeologist.

You saw Pat Ripley in the supermarket yesterday. She just moved here from England. She's a journalist.

You ran into Charles Paxton the other day. He was in your math class. He's a bank teller.

You got a letter from Liz Holt. She's living in Chile. She's a teacher.

56. I was in the neighborhood.

Kate Simmons stops by to see Doug at the recreation center.

1

Kate Hi, Doug! I see you got the job. Congratulations!

Doug Kate! What brings you here?

Kate I was in the neighborhood. One of my elderly clients lives around here. So, how's it going?

Doug Well, so far so good. Things are still a little confusing, or should I say, I'm a little confused. . . .

Kate Well, it's only your first week. Listen, tomorrow is Gloria Smith's last day and we're having a little party for her at the agency. You've met Gloria, haven't you?

Doug Let's see. . . . Gloria . . . is she the one who sits by the window?

Kate That's right—the one with the long red hair. Anyway, Mr. Dow wanted me to tell you to be sure and come.

Doug Oh, well, I'll definitely try to make it. What time should I be there?

Kate Oh, about a quarter to five. So, are you all settled?

Doug I wish. I'm still looking for an apartment. If you hear of anything . . .

Kate Actually, a good friend of mine, Terry Enders, just moved into a new building. I can ask her if there are any apartments there.

Doug Oh, thanks. That would be great. What's her name again?

Kate Terry . . . Terry Enders. Why, do you know her?

Doug No, I don't think I do. But the name rings a bell.

2. Figure it out

Say *True, False,* or *It doesn't say.*

1. This is the first time Kate has seen Doug since he got the job.
2. Doug doesn't know who Gloria is.
3. Doug has already met everyone at the Community Services Agency.
4. There are some empty apartments in Terry Enders's building.
5. Doug has worked at his new job less than a week.
6. Doug is staying in a hotel.

3. Listen in

Kate calls Terry about an apartment for Doug. Read Kate's part of the conversation below. Then, as you listen to Terry, put the sentences in the right order.

___ Yes, that's right. He just moved to Chicago.

_1_ Hello, Terry? This is Kate.

___ O.K., let me get a pencil. (*Returns with pencil*) O.K. . . .

___ What was the number again?

___ A friend of mine, Doug Lee, needs an apartment. Are there any in your building?

57. Your turn

**Eating customs differ from country to country. Describe
how each person is eating, using the words under each
picture. Then discuss these questions in groups.**

1. Where do you think these people are from?
2. Are any of these customs similar to yours?
3. Which customs are different from yours?
4. What are some of the eating customs in your country?
5. What other interesting eating customs have you seen?

right hand—left hand—lap

eat—chopsticks

eat—hands

peel an orange—knife—fork

How to say it

Practice the conversation.

A That chicken looks good, doesn't it?

B It really does.

A And you're hungry, aren't you?

B Yes, I am.

A Well, let's eat!

58.

Ask Diana Wilkins

If you've just arrived in the United States . . .

by Diana Wilkins

Before you read the column, read the statements in exercise 1 and decide if they are *True* or *False*. Then read the column to see if you were right.

DEAR DIANA:

I'm a visitor to the United States. I have met many people, and some of them have invited me to dinner at their homes. The trouble is that I always get nervous on these occasions. I'm afraid that I will do something that is inappropriate because I don't know the customs very well. Could you please tell me what some of the most important rules are?

—CONFUSED

DEAR CONFUSED:

Your reaction to dinner invitations is quite natural, and I have received many letters on this topic from other visitors. Therefore, I have made a list of some of the specific rules to follow:

- **If the dinner is informal, ask if you can bring something, such as something to drink or dessert.**
- **Arrive five to ten minutes late, but never early. Your host or hostess may still be getting ready.**
- **Take off your hat and coat as soon as you enter someone's home.**
- **Feel free to politely refuse food that you don't want. You can say, "No, thanks. I don't care for any."**
- **Put your napkin on your lap before you begin to eat.**
- **If there are a number of utensils, those farthest from the plate are supposed to be used first. The last utensils to be used will be on the inside.**
- **If you'd like a second helping of something, you should go ahead and accept the first time it is offered. Your host or hostess may not offer it again.**
- **Remember to thank your host or hostess when you leave. You should also telephone the next day to say thank you again.**

These are some of the basic guidelines, and, of course, they may vary with the situation. When in doubt, it is best to look at what the other people at the table are doing.

1. **Decide if the statements below are *True* or *False*, based on the information in the column.**

1. You should never bring dessert to a dinner.
2. You should arrive at least ten minutes early.
3. Take off your hat and coat when you enter someone's house.
4. One way to politely refuse food is to say, "No, thanks. I don't care for any."
5. You should leave the napkin on the table when you eat.
6. The last utensils to use will be the closest to your plate.
7. Don't accept an offer of food or drink until the offer has been made at least twice.
8. You should thank your host or hostess twice—when you leave and the next day.

2. **Discuss these questions.**

1. Which of the above rules are similar to customs in your own country?
2. Which ones are different?

FUNCTIONS/THEMES	LANGUAGE	FORMS
Talk about a vacation	I was bored most of the time. The restaurants were a little disappointing.	Present participles and past participles used as adjectives
Talk about places	You really ought to go to Brazil. You won't be disappointed.	*Ought to*
Talk about location Compass directions	It's in the southern part of the country. It's about 600 miles southwest of Rio de Janeiro.	
Offer, accept, and decline food and drink	Would anyone care for coffee? Here are some sandwiches. Help yourselves.	
Identify someone	Who's the woman standing behind Jack? She's someone (who, that) we met at the park.	Relative clauses

Preview the conversations.

Grand Canyon National Park, U.S.A.

Every minute of the day, the light changes the colors and form of this magnificent canyon of the Colorado River. Sunrises and sunsets are particularly spectacular. As much as 14 miles wide and about a mile deep, the canyon is home to at least 220 different species of birds and many other forms of wildlife.
 Located in the northwestern part of the state of Arizona, the park covers more than one million acres.

The South Rim of the canyon, open all year, has the greatest number of services and is the most popular area with tourists. The North Rim, blocked by heavy snows in winter, is open from approximately mid-May to late October. It is a 215-mile drive from one rim to the other. The South Rim has an altitude of about 7,000 feet; the North Rim is about 8,100 feet. The river is about 4,600 feet below the South Rim.

1. Read the article. Then choose a partner and discuss these questions:
   a. Would you like to visit the Grand Canyon?
   b. What places should visitors see in your country? Why?

2. Tell your partner about an interesting vacation that you've taken. Answer these questions:
   a. Where did you go on vacation?
   b. Where did you stay? (in a hotel? with friends? at a campsite?)
   c. What did you do?
   d. Did you have a good time?

59. Tell us about your trip.

 Molly and Jack have just come back from a trip to the Grand Canyon.
They've invited Sue and Ken over for dinner.

A

Jack Here's some apple pie that I made. Help yourselves.

Sue Oh, Jack, you've gone to so much trouble.

Jack It was no trouble at all.

Molly Would anyone care for coffee or tea?

Sue I'll have a cup of coffee, please.

Ken Make that two.

Molly Jack?

Jack I don't care for anything right now, thanks. Maybe later.

Sue Well, don't keep us in suspense. Tell us about your trip.

Molly I'd say it was the nicest vacation we've ever taken, wouldn't you, Jack?

Jack Absolutely. You really ought to go. You won't be disappointed.

Molly The scenery was spectacular.

Jack And the animal life was fascinating.

Molly Jack and I are very interested in wildlife.

Jack Would you like to see our slides? We just got them back today.

Ken Hmmm . . . it might be a little late for . . .

Sue Oh, of course. We'd love to see them.

B

(First slide)

Molly That's the camper that we rented.

Sue Did you have all your meals in it?

Molly We usually ate out at least once every day.

Jack To tell you the truth, the restaurants were a little disappointing.

(Second slide)

Molly Do you remember where this was, Jack?

Jack Sure. That's in Grand Canyon National Park.

Ken Where exactly is the Grand Canyon?

Jack It's in the northwestern part of Arizona, about 200 miles north of Phoenix.

(Third slide)

Sue Who's the woman who's standing behind Jack?

Molly Oh, the one with the hat? She's just someone we met at the park.

Jack Hmmm . . . I don't recognize her.

Molly Don't you remember? She's the one we had dinner with.

Jack Oh, yes. That's right.

(Fourth slide)

Molly Oh, look! That's the mule I rode in the canyon.

Sue That sounds exciting!

Figure it out

1. Listen to the conversations and choose *a* or *b*.

1. a. Molly and Jack thought the trip was boring.
   b. Molly and Jack thought the trip was the best one they've ever taken.

2. a. Sue seems interested in hearing about the trip.
   b. Ken really wants to see the slides.

2. Listen again and say *True, False,* or *It doesn't say.*

1. Jack bought the apple pie in a store.
2. Molly doesn't want anything to drink.
3. Ken wants two cups of coffee.
4. Molly and Jack ate all their meals in the camper.
5. Molly and Jack have their own camper.
6. Jack thought the restaurants were very good.

3. Choose *a* or *b*.

1. Here's a cake _____ I made.
   a. who
   b. that

2. I'm very interested _____ history.
   a. in
   b. with

3. Do you remember where _____?
   a. it was
   b. was it

4. I was _____ in the restaurants.
   a. disappointed
   b. disappointing

5. The trip was _____.
   a. fascinated
   b. fascinating

60. You won't be disappointed.

1 ▶ Listen to the conversation. A woman is asking a man about his vacation. Write *G* next to the things that were good about his trip and *B* next to the things that were bad.

__ the shopping
__ the weather
__ the museums
__ the beaches
__ the people
__ the restaurants

2 ▶ Listen to the two possible conversations.
▶ Work with a partner. Act out similar conversations about trips you have made.

A I just got back from my vacation.

B Oh, really? How was your trip?

A Great. The scenery was spectacular.
B It sounds wonderful.

A Not too good. I was bored most of the time.
B Oh, I'm sorry to hear that.

Some reasons why your trip was good

The scenery was spectacular.
The weather was fantastic.
The museums were fascinating.
The food was excellent.
The people were very friendly.

Some reasons why your trip was bad

I was bored most of the time.
There was nothing to do at night.
The restaurants were overpriced.
I was disappointed in the food.

---

3 ▶ Study the frames: Present participles and past participles used as adjectives

Present participles	
The movie was	**interesting.** **disappointing.** **boring.** **shocking.**

Past participles			
I was	**interested** **disappointed**	in	the movie.
	bored **shocked**	by	

4 ▶ Read the column in *Literary News*. Then fill in each blank with an appropriate participle from the box. Use a preposition where necessary.

The historical parts were very interesting, but . . .

boring	bored (by)
depressing	depressed (by)
disappointing	disappointed (in)
exciting	excited (by)
fascinating	fascinated (by)
interesting	interested (in)
shocking	shocked (by)

The Readers' Corner

Here are some of our readers' opinions of Mary Harmon's new book, *The Village Sleeps*.

"The historical parts were very _____ , but frankly, I was a little _____ the ending." **(Terry Roma, Boston)**

"I was a little _____ at first, but the third chapter was so _____ I couldn't put it down." **(Emma Smith, Winnipeg)**

"It was too _____ . I'd rather read something optimistic." **(Oscar Garcia, Mexico City)**

"I was _____ the strong language! Not a book for our young people." **(Glen McMahon, Dallas)**

5

► **Tony recently took a trip to Brazil. He's trying to convince his friend Roy to go there. Listen to the conversation and practice it with a partner.**

Tony You really ought to go to Brazil. You won't be disappointed.

Roy Tell me something about it.

Tony Well, the scenery is magnificent, and the people are very friendly. Brazilian food is fantastic, too.

6

► **Work with a partner. Imagine your partner has never been to your country and is planning a vacation. Try to convince him or her to take a trip to your country, region, or city. Start with:**

You really ought to go to . . .

7

► **Roy wants to know more about Tony's trip. Listen to the conversation and practice it with a partner.**

► **Work with a partner. Act out similar conversations about the exact location of your city, town, or neighborhood.**

Roy Where were you in Brazil?

Tony Mostly in Porto Alegre.

Roy Where exactly is that?

Tony It's in the southern part of the country. It's about 600 miles southwest of Rio de Janeiro.

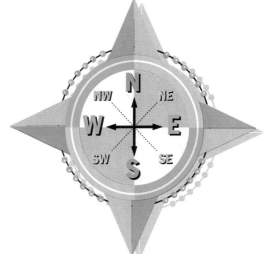

Some locations		
in the	northern southern eastern western central	part
on the (Atlantic) coast		south [saʊθ]

61. Would anyone care for coffee?

1 ▶ **Listen to the conversations. Does the person accept or decline the offer?**

> Oh, thanks, but I'm on a diet.

	ACCEPT	DECLINE
1.	_____	_____
2.	_____	_____
3.	_____	_____
4.	_____	_____

2 ▶ **Listen to the conversation and practice it in groups of three.**
▶ **Act out similar conversations, using the food and drinks in the pictures.**

A Would anyone care for coffee?
B I'll have a cup, please.
C No, thanks. I'm trying to cut down on coffee.
A Here are some sandwiches. Help yourselves.
C Oh, thank you. You've gone to so much trouble.
A It was no trouble at all.

(a cup of) coffee

a sandwich

some chocolate cake

some snacks

some cookies

some tea

Other ways to say it	Some ways to decline
Would you care for . . .? Would you like . . .? Do you want . . .?	I don't care for anything right now, thanks. Oh, thanks, but I'm on a diet. No, thanks. I'm trying to cut down (on caffeine, sugar, fat, etc.). Thanks, but I'm not really hungry/thirsty.

3 ▶ **Work in groups of three. Play these roles.**

Student A   Students B and C are visiting you at home. Offer them something to eat and drink. If anyone declines an offer, try offering him or her something else.

Student B   You and Student C are visiting Student A's home. You're really hungry and thirsty. Everything Student A offers you looks delicious. Accept everything that Student A offers.

Student C   You and Student B are visiting Student A's home. You really don't want anything to eat or drink right now. Politely decline everything that Student A offers.

62. He's someone I went to school with.

1 ▶ Listen to the conversation. Can you identify John, Yong Hee, Toshi, Marie, and Lisa in the picture?

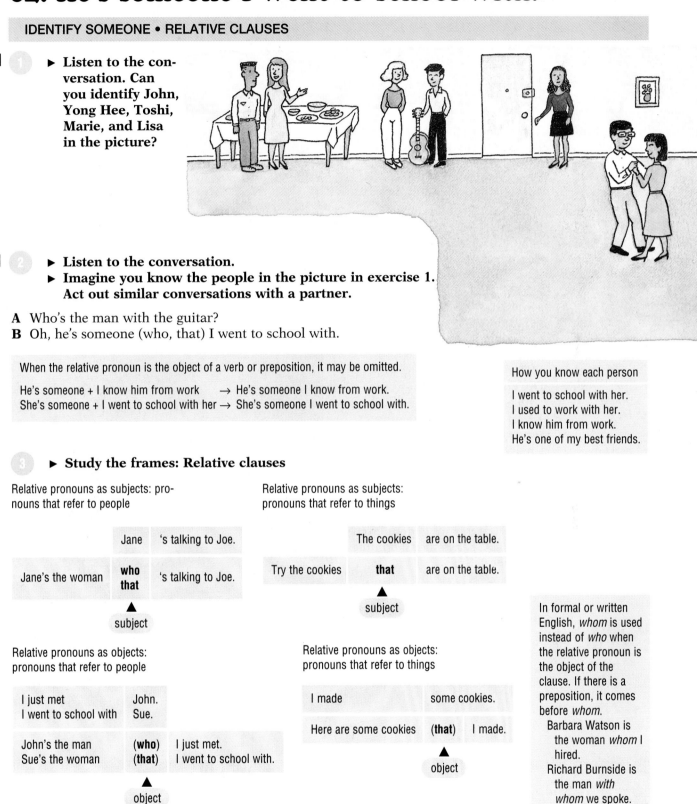

2 ▶ Listen to the conversation.
▶ Imagine you know the people in the picture in exercise 1. Act out similar conversations with a partner.

A Who's the man with the guitar?
B Oh, he's someone (who, that) I went to school with.

When the relative pronoun is the object of a verb or preposition, it may be omitted.

He's someone + I know him from work → He's someone I know from work.
She's someone + I went to school with her → She's someone I went to school with.

How you know each person

I went to school with her.
I used to work with her.
I know him from work.
He's one of my best friends.

3 ▶ **Study the frames: Relative clauses**

Relative pronouns as subjects: pronouns that refer to people

Jane	's talking to Joe.

Jane's the woman	**who** **that**	's talking to Joe.

▲ subject

Relative pronouns as subjects: pronouns that refer to things

The cookies	are on the table.

Try the cookies	**that**	are on the table.

▲ subject

Relative pronouns as objects: pronouns that refer to people

| I just met | John. |
| I went to school with | Sue. |

| John's the man | **(who)** | I just met. |
| Sue's the woman | **(that)** | I went to school with. |

▲ object

Relative pronouns as objects: pronouns that refer to things

I made	some cookies.

Here are some cookies	**(that)**	I made.

▲ object

In formal or written English, *whom* is used instead of *who* when the relative pronoun is the object of the clause. If there is a preposition, it comes before *whom*.
Barbara Watson is the woman *whom* I hired.
Richard Burnside is the man *with whom* we spoke.

4 ▶ **Complete the second sentence in each pair with a relative clause.**

1. I just met John.
   John's the man _(that) I just met_ .

2. I saw a great movie called *Rashomon* yesterday.
   Rashomon is a great movie _____ .

3. I got some cake at the bakery.
   Here's some cake _____ .

4. We met Lily on a trip to Taiwan.
   Lily's the woman _____ .

Unit 9 **97**

63. He hasn't been himself.

Mr. and Mrs. Enders are visiting their daughters, Laura and Terry, who live in Chicago. They've all gone to the Museum of Science and Industry.

1

Mr. Enders	This is one of the finest museums I've ever been to, and I've been to a lot of museums. It's a shame Chuck couldn't make it. We've seen so little of him this trip.
Laura	Well, he hasn't been himself lately.
Mr. Enders	Is he still upset about the job?
Laura	Yes, he was really disappointed.
Mr. Enders	He can't go on being depressed forever. He has to start looking for something else.
Laura	Oh, he has. Actually, there *is* one possibility, but I'm not too excited about it.
Mr. Enders	Why not? It's not a good job?
Laura	Oh, no, it's a great job—very similar to the one he didn't get. It's an even larger recreation program, but it's in Los Angeles. Chuck has a brother who lives there.
Mr. Enders	Does it look promising?
Laura	No, I really don't think he'll get it, and, well, I know this sounds selfish, but in a way I'm relieved. I mean, L.A. is two thousand miles from here.

2. Figure it out

Say *True, False,* or *It doesn't say.*

1. Laura's parents have met Chuck before.
2. Chuck has been too depressed to start looking for another job.
3. Laura hopes Chuck will get the job in Los Angeles.
4. Chuck's brother told him about the job.
5. Laura doesn't want Chuck to move so far away.

3. Listen in

Terry and Mrs. Enders join Laura and Mr. Enders. Read the statements below. Then listen to the conversation and choose *a* or *b*.

The Enders family is going to eat
   a. at Laura's house.
   b. at a restaurant.

64. Your turn

Work with a partner. Moonlight Travel Agency sponsored a "Win a Trip" contest, and you and your partner have just won a vacation for two. You can choose to go to any one of the four cities below. Discuss the attractions of each place, and decide where you will take your vacation.

ATHENS, Greece
Attractions:
★ Ancient Greece — the Acropolis, the Parthenon
★ nightlife — music and dancing
★ shopping — clothing, rugs, and crafts
★ museums and galleries

ROME, Italy
Attractions:
★ Ancient Rome — the Colosseum, the Roman Forum
★ the Vatican
★ art museums
★ delicious food

CAIRO, Egypt
Attractions:
★ the Pyramids
★ shopping—crafts, jewelry, and cotton clothing
★ fascinating culture
★ 3,000 years of history

RIO DE JANEIRO, Brazil
Attractions:
★ nightlife—great music and dancing
★ shopping—jewelry and crafts
★ Copacabana Beach
★ excursions to beautiful rain forests

How to say it

Practice the words. Then practice the conversation.

interesting [íntrəstɪŋ]   fascinating [fǽsənetɪŋ]   exciting [ɪksáɪtɪŋ]   disappointing [dɪsə pɔ́ɪntɪŋ]

A How was your trip?
B Great. There were so many interesting things to see, and the museums were fascinating.
A It sounds exciting. How was the food?
B Well, a little disappointing, but not too bad.

65.

Ancient Greece

Before you read the encyclopedia entries, look at the pictures and tell what you know about them.

The Acropolis

ACROPOLIS (the)

A rocky hill in the center of Athens, **Greece,** on which many other temples and important **buildings** were built. After many old buildings on the Acropolis were destroyed in 480 B.C., the Athenians, under the **leadership** of Pericles, **built** new temples. One of these constructions, the Parthenon, was built in honor of the goddess **Athena,** for whom the city of Athens was named. (See *Parthenon, Pericles*)

The Parthenon

PARTHENON (the)

An ancient **Greek** temple in **Athens,** built between 447 and 432 B.C., during the time when Pericles was the leader. The temple overlooks the city from a hill called the Acropolis. Dedicated to the goddess Athena, the marble temple had **sculptures** showing scenes of her life. This **construction**—which over time served as a church and a mosque—is possibly the best example of ancient Greek **architecture** even though only ruins remain today. (See *Acropolis, Pericles*)

Marble scupture of Pericles

PERICLES (490?–429 B.C.)

An ancient **Athenian** who became **leader** of the **government** in 460 B.C. He **governed** Athens for more than thirty years. During his rule, known as the "Age of Pericles," he became a patron of the arts and wanted to make Athens the most beautiful city in Greece. He had **architects** and **sculptors construct** and decorate temples and other buildings, among them the Parthenon, built in honor of the goddess Athena.
(See *Acropolis, Parthenon*)

1. **Read the encyclopedia entries. Then find each of the words below and say whether it is used as a *noun*, a *verb*, or an *adjective* in the article.**

1. Athenian *noun*
2. Athens
3. Athena
4. government
5. governed
6. architects
7. architecture
8. sculptors
9. sculptures
10. construct
11. construction
12. Greek
13. Greece
14. leader
15. leadership
16. buildings
17. built

2. **Discuss these questions.**

1. Who are some famous leaders in the history of your country? What are they famous for?
2. What are some important buildings and constructions in your country? Where are they located?

PREVIEW

FUNCTIONS/THEMES	LANGUAGE	FORMS
Talk about the size of an apartment	I'm calling about the apartment you advertised. Could you tell me more about it? The living room's eighteen by twenty-three feet.	
Ask about apartments	Does it say how much it is? Could you tell me what floor it's on?	Embedded questions
Talk about transportation	Could you tell me which bus goes to the Fine Arts Museum? Do you know how often the Number 1 bus runs during rush hour? Every five minutes or so.	
Talk about location	Do you know where Oak Street is? It's off Washington, near the park.	Prepositions
State a preference	I'd rather live in an older building. I'd rather not live in a modern building.	*I'd rather* and *I'd rather not*

Preview the conversations.

Lge 2 BR on quiet st nr transp. Avail immed. $800 + utils. 555-9462 eves.

Tired of city living? 1 BR apt in mod bldg, 20 mi N of town in lovely sub setting. 555-5470

3 rm mod apt, great loc. $750. 555-2483

1 BR apt nr buses. Reasonable rent. 555-5430

1. Read the ads. With a partner, try to figure out what these abbreviations mean. You will find the answers on page 165.

apt	eves	mod	st
avail	immed	N	sub
bldg	lge	nr	transp
BR	loc	rm	utils

2. What are some questions people ask when they call about an apartment? Make a list.

66. Is it still available?

Debbie is looking for an apartment, and her friend Hiro is helping her.

A

Hiro How does this sound? "Sunny one-bedroom near transportation, centrally located. . . ."

Debbie It's just what I'm looking for. Does it say how much it is?

Hiro It's $850 a month including utilities.

Debbie I can't afford to pay that much.

Hiro Maybe you should look for a roommate.

Debbie No, I'd rather have my own place. Now here's a one-bedroom for $650 a month on Oak Street. Do you have any idea where that is?

Hiro It's off Washington, near the park.

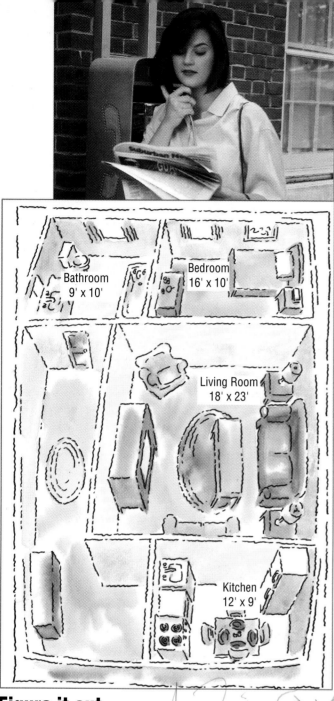

Bathroom
9' x 10'

Bedroom
16' x 10'

Living Room
18' x 23'

Kitchen
12' x 9'

Landlady Hello?

Debbie Hello. I'm calling about the apartment you advertised. Is it still available?

Landlady Yes, it is.

Debbie Could you tell me more about it?

Landlady Sure. There are three rooms and a bath. The living room's pretty large—about eighteen by twenty-three feet. The bedroom and kitchen are smaller. Oh, and there's parking available. Do you have a car?

Debbie Yes, but I'd rather not drive to work. How close is it to public transportation?

Landlady The Number 1 bus stops a block away.

Debbie Do you happen to know how often it runs during rush hour?

Landlady Every five minutes or so.

Debbie It sounds perfect. What floor is it on?

Landlady The first floor.

Debbie Hmmm . . . that's a problem. I'd rather not live on the first floor.

Landlady Well, that's all I have for the time being, but I will have a studio apartment on the third floor in the near future.

Debbie How soon will it be available?

Landlady November 1st.

Debbie Oh, well, I really can't wait that long. But thanks anyway.

Figure it out

1. **Listen to the conversations and choose the correct answers.**

1. a. Debbie calls about a three-bedroom apartment.
   b. Debbie wants a one-bedroom apartment.

2. a. Debbie wants an apartment very soon.
   b. The landlady wants to rent the apartment sooner than Debbie can move in.

2. **Listen again and say *True, False,* or *It doesn't say.***

1. Debbie wants to live alone.
2. The Oak Street apartment is $650 a month with utilities.
3. Washington Street is near the park.
4. Debbie doesn't drive.
5. Debbie doesn't want an apartment on the first floor.

3. **Find another way to say it.**

1. fairly big   *pretty large*
2. now
3. fairly soon
4. about every five minutes

4. **Match.**

1. How soon?   a. Every five minutes.
2. How often?   b. $650 a month.
3. How close?   c. November 1st.
4. How much?   d. Eighteen by twenty-three.
5. How big?   e. The next block.

67. Could you tell me more about it?

1 ▶ **A man is calling about an apartment he saw advertised in the newspaper. Listen to the conversation and complete the information about the apartment.**

A I'm calling about the apartment you advertised. Is it still available?
B Yes, it is.
A Could you tell me more about it?
B Well, there are _____ rooms. The _____ is fairly large—about _____ by _____ feet.
A How big is the _____ ?
B It's a little _____ than the kitchen—about twenty feet by twenty feet.
A And what about the _____ ?
B Oh, it's sort of small—about twelve by fifteen feet.
A That doesn't sound too bad. When can I see it?

▶ **Imagine you have advertised your own apartment in a newspaper. Act out similar conversations with a partner.**

2 ▶ **Work with a partner. Play these roles.**

Student A You are trying to find an apartment, and you see this ad in a newspaper. Call Student B and ask about the size of the apartment.

Student B You put this ad in the newspaper. Student A calls you and asks about the apartment. Answer Student A's questions, using the floor plan on page 103.

> **APARTMENT FOR RENT**
> 1 BR near transp. Available immediately.
> Call 555-0859 eves.

3 ▶ **Listen to the conversation and practice it with a partner.**
▶ **Act out similar conversations, using the ads and your own ideas.**

A Great Option Rentals. May I help you?
B Yes. I'm calling about the studio apartment you advertised in *Community News*. Could you please tell me how much it costs?
A Yes. It's $600 a month.
B And could you tell me what floor it's on?
A It's on the second floor.

utilities (utils.) = heat (and hot water), gas, and electricity	A studio apartment has no separate bedroom.

> **GREAT OPTION RENTALS**
> **555-1003**
> Sunny 1 BR nr transp. centrally located. $725 a month, including utils.
>
> Lge studio in mod bldg, nr shops & transp. Reasonably priced, avail 12/1.
>
> 2 BR on quiet st, older bldg. $825, 4th fl.

4 ▶ **Study the frames: Embedded questions**

| Where is it? |
| How much does it cost? |
| How soon will it be available? |

Does it say	**where it is?**
Do you know	**how much it costs?**
Could you tell me	**how soon it will be available?**

| What's included in the rent? |
| Which bus runs near the apartment? |

| Do you know | **what's included in the rent?** |
| Could you tell me | **which bus runs near the apartment?** |

When the question word is the subject of the embedded question, the word order is the same as in a simple subject question.

5 ▶ **Listen to the conversation and practice it with a partner.**
▶ **Act out similar conversations, using the ads in exercise 3.**

A How does this sound? "Sunny one-bedroom near transportation, centrally located. . . ."
B Does it say how much it is?
A It's $725 a month.
B Does it say what's included in the rent?
A No, it doesn't.

Does it say. . .

how much it is?
what's included in the rent?
what floor it's on?
where it's located?
how close it is to transportation?
how soon it will be available?

6 ▶ **Work with a partner. Play these roles.**

Student A Call Great Option Rentals about an apartment in one of the ads in exercise 3. Ask questions that weren't answered in the ad. Begin some of your questions with *Could you please tell me . . .?*

Student B You work at Great Option Rentals. Answer Student A's questions, using the information below.

One bedroom: 348 Crescent St.
Apt. 1A
First floor. Available first of month.
One block from bus.
$725, including all utils.

Two bedroom: 20 Maple St.
Apt. 4
Rent includes heat, but other utilities extra.
Available immediately. Fourth floor.
10 min to bus stop. $825

Studio: 413 Walnut St. Apt. 2B
$600 a month, utilities extra.
Second floor. Two blocks from buses and shops. Available 12/1.

68. Do you know how often the bus runs?

TALK ABOUT TRANSPORTATION • EMBEDDED QUESTIONS

1 ▶ Listen to the conversation. Which bus is the man asking about?

BUSES
approximate frequency in minutes

No.	Rush Hour	Day	Night	Sat.	Sun.
1	5	10	20	12	12
2	6	15	25	15	20
3	12	15	30	30	45
4	7	10	15	15	15

2 ▶ Listen to the two possible conversations.
▶ Act out similar conversations with a partner, using the information in the bus schedule.

A Do you know how often the Number 1 bus runs during rush hour?

B Oh, every five minutes or so.　　**B** Sorry, I have no idea.

Some time periods

during rush hour
during the day
at night
on weekends

Other ways to say it

about every five minutes

Could you tell me which bus goes to the Fine Arts Museum?

3 ▶ Listen to the two possible conversations.
▶ Work with a partner. Act out similar conversations about how to get to different places in your city or town.

A Could you tell me which bus goes to the Fine Arts Museum?

B Well, the Number 1 stops a block away.　　**B** Sorry, I don't know.

TALK ABOUT LOCATION • PREPOSITIONS

4 ▶ Look at the map and match the streets with their locations.

1. Lincoln
2. Pine
3. Jefferson
4. Gate

a. crosses Washington Street.
b. is parallel to Washington, on the other side of the park.
c. is off Washington, not far from the park.
d. is off Oak.

5 ▶ Listen to the conversation.
▶ Work with a partner. Act out similar conversations about the streets on the map.
▶ Have conversations about the locations of streets in your city, town, or neighborhood.

A Do you know where Oak Street is?
B It's off Washington, near the park.
A And do you have any idea where Pine Street is?
B No, I'm afraid I don't.

69. I'd rather not live in a modern building.

1 ▶ Louisa is talking to a real estate agent about renting an apartment. Listen to the conversation and check (√) her preferences.

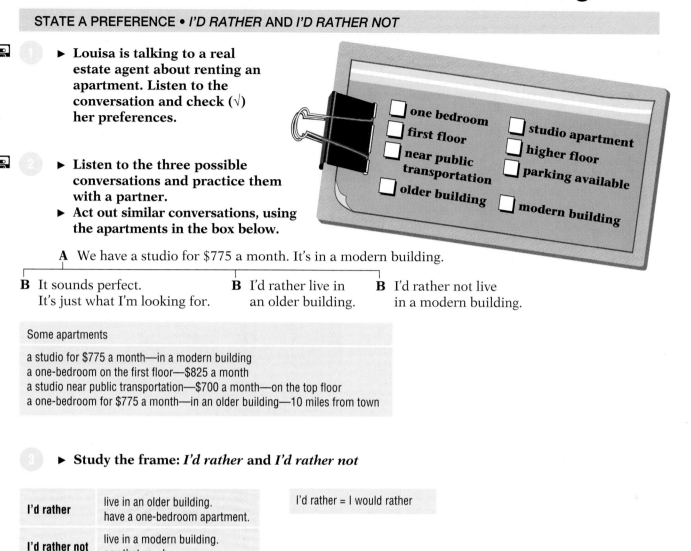

☐ one bedroom
☐ first floor
☐ near public transportation
☐ older building

☐ studio apartment
☐ higher floor
☐ parking available
☐ modern building

2 ▶ Listen to the three possible conversations and practice them with a partner.
▶ Act out similar conversations, using the apartments in the box below.

A We have a studio for $775 a month. It's in a modern building.

B It sounds perfect. It's just what I'm looking for.

B I'd rather live in an older building.

B I'd rather not live in a modern building.

Some apartments

a studio for $775 a month—in a modern building
a one-bedroom on the first floor—$825 a month
a studio near public transportation—$700 a month—on the top floor
a one-bedroom for $775 a month—in an older building—10 miles from town

3 ▶ Study the frame: *I'd rather* and *I'd rather not*

I'd rather	live in an older building. have a one-bedroom apartment.
I'd rather not	live in a modern building. pay that much.

I'd rather = I would rather

4 ▶ Listen to the conversation and practice it with a partner.
▶ Act out similar conversations, using the activities in the pictures below and your own ideas.

A Why don't we watch a movie on TV tonight?
B I'd rather watch the soccer game.

watch a movie on TV   go out to eat   go to a rock concert   play cards

70. It's not quite what I had in mind.

Doug is talking with Dan Harper and Gloria Smith at Gloria's going-away party. He is telling them about his new apartment.

1

Dan Kate tells me you found an apartment.

Doug Yes. As a matter of fact, she's the one who told me about it. A friend of hers lives in the same building.

Dan What's it like?

Doug It's a studio—one big room with a kitchenette. I'd rather have a one-bedroom, but at the prices they're asking, I can't afford it, at least not for the time being.

Gloria I know what you mean. Apartments cost an arm and a leg these days. I hope we can find something inexpensive in New York. Is your apartment in pretty good shape at least?

Doug Yes, it's in a new building. Actually, it's not quite what I had in mind. I'd rather have something less modern, but I'm lucky to have found this. And the location's great.

Dan Where is it exactly?

Doug On Wilson, right off Broadway.

Dan Oh, I know where that is. That *is* a good location. Are you all moved in and settled?

Doug For the most part. The walls are kind of bare, though. Does either of you know where I can get some posters around here?

Dan Not offhand.

Gloria Ask Kate. She'd know that kind of thing.

2. Figure it out

Say *True, False,* or *It doesn't say.*

1. Doug looked for an apartment for a long time and found just what he wanted.
2. Doug thinks the rents in Chicago are expensive.
3. Doug doesn't have enough money for a one-bedroom apartment.
4. Dan has lived in Chicago for a few years.
5. Gloria is going to move away from Chicago.
6. Doug hasn't moved into his new apartment yet.
7. Doug has finished decorating his apartment.

3. Listen in

Gloria is telling Mr. Dow and Kate Simmons about her future plans. Read the questions below. Then listen to the conversation and choose *a* or *b*.

1. Why are Gloria and her husband, John, moving to New York?
   a. John has a new job.
   b. Gloria is going back to school.

2. How soon do Gloria and John have to be in New York?
   a. In about two weeks.
   b. In a few days.

71. Your turn

Where would you like to live?

Discuss these questions in groups.

1. If you could live in any one of these homes, which one would you choose? Why?
2. Are any of these homes similar to ones you might find in your country? Which ones?
3. What type of home do you live in now? Describe it.

Here are some things that are important to some people when they choose a place to live. In groups, discuss which of these are most important to you. Can you add to the list?

- close to work
- close to public transportation
- attractive building
- modern kitchen and bathroom

- reasonable rent or purchase price
- available parking
- plenty of space
- close to shopping

How to say it

Practice the conversation.

A I just saw a nice apartment.

B Really? Where is it?

A Next to the Sunset Theater. Do you know where that is?

B Sure. That's a great neighborhood.

HOMELESSNESS—
What Can Be Done?

"Home is the place where, when you
have to go there,
They have to take you in."
— **Robert Frost, American Poet**

Before you read the article, look at the photographs. Who do you think these people are? How did they get into this condition? How many homeless people are there in the world today?

At one time there was a romantic vision of homeless wanderers who lived carefree lives and answered to no one. Home might be a park bench or an empty boxcar on a train heading to some unknown place. They were easy to ignore—people felt they chose the life they wanted.

But today homeless people are not easy to ignore. They are everywhere—in large and small cities, all over the world. According to the United Nations, there are over 100 million homeless people worldwide. Where are they living? In places like abandoned buildings, shelters, bus and train stations, subways, and city streets. Large cities such as New York, London, and Bombay (to name a few) can barely cope with the large numbers of people living on the streets.

It is impossible to estimate the exact number of homeless people because the conditions of homelessness vary. Sometimes people are temporarily without a home because of a fire or a hurricane, for example. Sometimes people are forced out of their homes because they can't pay the rent. Others might be living on the streets for years. It is not easy to count them. Nor is it easy to describe a typical homeless person, for the picture has changed over the years and differs from place to place.

What are the causes of homelessness? For some, it is simply a lack of affordable housing. Many of the homeless have lost their jobs and are poor. Many others have problems with drugs or alcohol. Some have left home because the conditions there were so bad. Others are mentally ill, discharged from hospitals with nowhere to go. They have no family and no one they can turn to.

What can be done? The most promising suggestions are those that will attack the problems that made people homeless in the first place. Governments can put more money into building low-cost housing. The mentally ill need special places to live, with supervision, like group homes. People with addictions need places where they can be helped to overcome them. Job training may help some people to get new skills and find work. But all of these suggestions cost money, which cities are hard pressed to come up with as they try to cope with new waves of homelessness. Is there an end to this problem in sight? Not anytime soon.

---

1. Read the article. Then answer these questions.

1. Why is it difficult to ignore the homeless today?
2. What are some of the causes of homelessness discussed in the article?
3. What are some suggested solutions to the problem of homelessness?

2. Discuss these questions in a group.

1. Is homelessness a problem in your country?
2. If so, has it gotten worse in the past few years?
3. What do you think is the cause?
4. What do you think can be done about homelessness?

FUNCTIONS/THEMES	LANGUAGE	FORMS
Talk about plans	Do you have any plans for the weekend? It depends on the weather. If it's nice, I'll go to the beach.	Conditional sentences
Make an offer	If you need a ride to the airport, I'll be happy to drive you.	
Talk about a trip	I'm thinking of flying, but it depends on how much it costs.	Embedded questions
Ask for clarification Make a comparison	Could you speak a little louder?	The comparative of adverbs
Give an excuse	How come? I couldn't get a later flight.	*Couldn't*
Make a reservation	I'd like some information about morning flights from Bangkok to Taipei.	

Preview the conversations.

Look at the timetable. All of the flights leave from Chicago. Then discuss these questions with a partner.

1. What time does Flight 416 leave Chicago? What time does in arrive in Toronto?
2. How long does Flight 412 take to get from Chicago to Montreal?
3. Do you have to change planes on the morning flight between Chicago and Ottawa?
4. Do they serve any meals on Flight 406?
5. Does Flight 416 from Chicago to Toronto make any stops?

From CHICAGO

Flight No.	Lv.	Arr.	Via	Meal
To MONTREAL				
406/402	7:00a	11:35a	TORONTO	B
412	1:00p	5:00p		L
422	4:00p	8:35p		D
To OTTAWA				
416/404	11:00a	3:40p	TORONTO	L
410	2:00p	5:45p		S
To TORONTO				
406	7:00a	10:26a		B
416	11:00a	2:26p		L
418/444	2:00p	5:09p	DETROIT	S
424/436	6:00p	10:09p	DETROIT	D

Meal Service
B = Breakfast L = Lunch D = Dinner S = Snack

73. It depends . . .

Bob Ross and Ann Watson both live in Chicago and work in the same office. They are talking about their plans for the long holiday weekend.

A

Bob Any plans for the long weekend?

Ann It depends on the weather. If it's nice, I'll probably go camping. But if it isn't, maybe I'll just stay home and clean my apartment. It could certainly use it. How about you?

Bob I'm going to Toronto.

Ann Oh, is that where you're from?

Bob No, that's where my parents live now. I grew up in Ottawa.

Ann How are you getting there?

Bob I'm thinking of flying, but it depends on how much it costs. If it's too expensive, I'll take the bus.

Ann Well, listen, if you need a ride to the airport, let me know. I'll be happy to drive you, if I'm around.

Bob Oh, thanks. That's really nice of you.

Mr. Ross Hello?

Bob Hello, Dad?

Mr. Ross Bob! We've been expecting your call. (*To his wife*) It's Bob.

Mrs. Ross Find out when he's coming.

Mr. Ross When are you coming?

Bob Saturday at four.

Mr. Ross (*To his wife*) He's coming on Saturday at four.

Mrs. Ross Not until four? How come?

Mr. Ross Why so late?

Bob I couldn't get an earlier flight.

Mr. Ross (*To his wife*) He couldn't get an earlier flight.

Bob Have you heard from Carol?

Mr. Ross Have I heard what?

Bob Have you heard from Carol?

Mr. Ross Yes. She can't come until Saturday night. She couldn't get the day off from the hospital.

Bob Oh, that's too bad.

Mr. Ross Bob, I can hardly hear what you're saying. Could you speak a little louder?

Bob I said that's too bad. Listen, this is a bad connection. It must be this phone. Give my love to Mom and I'll see you both on Saturday.

Mr. Ross O.K., I will. See you Saturday.

Figure it out

1. **Listen to the conversations and choose the correct answers.**

1. a. Ann cleaned her apartment yesterday.
   b. Ann's apartment needs to be cleaned.

2. a. Ann might go camping over the weekend.
   b. Ann will definitely stay home over the weekend.

3. a. Bob couldn't get a flight to Toronto.
   b. Bob is thinking about flying to Toronto.

4. a. Taking the bus to Toronto is probably cheaper than flying.
   b. Taking the bus to Toronto is probably more expensive than flying.

5. a. Carol is in the hospital.
   b. Carol works at a hospital.

6. a. Carol can't come over on Saturday.
   b. Carol has to work on Saturday.

2. **Choose *a* or *b*.**

1. Find out _____ .
   a. when is he coming
   b. when he's coming

2. It depends on _____ .
   a. how long does it take
   b. how long it takes

3. If _____ a ride, let me know.
   a. you need
   b. you'll need

4. I tried to get an earlier flight, _____ .
   a. but I can't
   b. but I couldn't

74. If it's nice, I'll go to the beach.

TALK ABOUT PLANS • MAKE AN OFFER • CONDITIONAL SENTENCES

1
▶ Listen to the conversation and practice it with a partner.
▶ Act out similar conversations, using your own information.

A Do you have any plans for the weekend?
B It depends on the weather. If it's nice, I'll go to the beach. If it isn't, I'll probably stay home and catch up on some reading.

What if . . .	Some things to do in bad weather
it's nice?	do some errands
it isn't (nice)?	watch TV
it rains?	stay home and clean the house
it doesn't (rain)?	catch up on some reading

If it's nice, I'll go to the beach.

If it isn't, I'll probably stay home and catch up on some reading.

2
▶ What offers are these people making? Complete the conversations with the offers in the box.
▶ Listen to check your work.
▶ Practice the conversations with a partner.

Make an offer
I'll be happy to…
drive you.
come over and give you a hand.
lend you mine.

1. **A** I'm moving into my new house tomorrow.
   B Well, if you need some help, _____ .

2. **A** I'm catching a flight to Montreal right after work.
   B Well, listen, if you need a ride to the airport, _____ _____ .

3. **A** I'm going camping this weekend, but I don't have a sleeping bag.
   B Well, if you need one, _____ _____ .

3
▶ Study the frame:
Conditional sentences

	Present tense	Future tense
If	the weather **is** good, it **isn't** too cool,	we**'ll have** a picnic. I**'ll go** to the beach.
	it **rains**, it **doesn't clear up**,	we **won't go** camping. I **won't play** tennis.

4
▶ Complete each statement, using your own information.

1. If it's nice this weekend, *I'll go to the beach* .
2. If I don't have much work tonight, _____ .
3. _____ , I'll answer some letters.
4. _____ , I probably won't go out this weekend.
5. If it doesn't rain tomorrow, _____ .
6. If I can save enough money, _____ .
7. _____ , I'll stay home and read a book.
8. If I learn to speak English fluently, _____ .

75. It depends on how much it costs.

1 ▶ **Listen to the conversation and practice it with a partner.**
▶ **Act out similar conversations, using your own information.**

A What are you doing this weekend?
B I'm taking the kids to Disneyland.
A Oh, really? How are you getting there?
B We might fly, but it depends on how much it costs. If it's
too expensive, we'll take the bus.

Some questions
How much does it cost? (How much is it?)
How long does it take? (How long is the trip?)
What time does the flight/train/bus leave?

2 ▶ **Study the frames: Embedded questions**

When is he coming?
How long does it take?
How long is he staying?

Find out	**when he's coming**.
It depends on	**how long it takes**.
Ask him	**how long he's staying**.

3 ▶ **Change these questions to embedded questions.**

1. Where are they going this weekend?   *Find out where they're going this weekend.*
2. How are they getting there?
3. How long is the trip?
4. Where are they staying?
5. When are they coming back?

4 ▶ **Work in groups of three. Play these roles.**

Student A A friend (Student B) is visiting you at home
when another friend (Student C) calls you from college for
the first time. Ask Student C the questions that Student B
suggests.

Student B You're visiting Student A when a friend
(Student C) who has gone away to college calls Student A.
Tell Student A what questions to ask Student C on the phone.

Student C You have recently gone to college. You're calling
a friend (Student A) for the first time from college.
Answer Student A's questions.

Ask her how she's doing.

B *Ask _____ how
he/she is doing.*
A *How are you doing?*
C *I'm fine.*
B *Find out . . .*

Some questions
How is he/she doing?
What classes is he/she taking?
How does he/she like the classes?
What's the weather like?
When is he/she coming home for a visit?

76. Could you speak a little louder?

1 ▶ **Listen to the conversation and practice it with a partner.**

A Have you finished the homework?
B Could you speak a little louder, please?
A HAVE YOU FINISHED THE HOMEWORK?

Could you speak . . .

louder?
slower?
more clearly?

2 ▶ **Work with a partner. Act out similar conversations to the one in exercise 1. Student A: Think of a question to ask Student B. Ask your question very softly, very fast, or very indistinctly. Student B: Ask for clarification.**

3 ▶ **Study the frames: The comparative of adverbs**

Can you come a little	**sooner**?	One syllable:	More than one syllable:	But:
I'll try to drive	**more carefully**.	Adverb + *er*	*More* or *less* + adverb	well → better badly → worse early → earlier

4 ▶ **What are these people saying? Complete the sentences with the comparative form of the adverbs in the box. There may be more than one possible answer.**

badly	early	loud (or loudly)	soon
carefully	fast	often	well
clearly	late	slow (or slowly)	

1. I used to speak Spanish _____ , but I've forgotten a lot.

2. I haven't finished my homework yet. Can I meet you a little _____ ?

3. Could you write this _____ , please? I can't read the name and address very well.

4. I'm sorry I couldn't get here _____ . The traffic was terrible.

5. Could you speak _____ , please? I can't hear you with all the noise.

5 ▶ **Talk to your classmates. Tell them about things you used to do differently than you do now.**

I used to get up earlier than I do now. / I speak English better than I used to.

77. I couldn't get a later flight.

1 ▶ Complete each conversation with an excuse from the box.
▶ Listen to check your work.
▶ Act out similar conversations with a partner. Use your own information.

Some excuses	
I couldn't	get tickets for Friday night. get a later flight. find a baby-sitter.

1. **A** When are you coming?
   B Saturday morning, about nine.
   A So early? How come?
   B _____ .

2. **A** I got tickets for the play on Saturday night.
   B I thought you wanted to go Friday.
   A I did, but _____ . They were sold out.

3. **A** Did you go out last night?
   B No, I stayed home and watched TV.
   A How come?
   B _____ .

MAKE A RESERVATION

2 ▶ Listen to the conversation and practice it with a partner.

A Pacific Airlines. May I help you?
B Yes, I'd like some information about morning flights from Bangkok to Taipei. Could you please tell me how long the flight takes?
A It depends on when you fly. If you leave at 6:30 in the morning, it takes about three-and-a-half hours.
B I'd rather not leave that early.
A Well, there's a flight at 8:30 A.M. But there's a stopover, so it takes a little longer.
B Do I have to change planes?
A No, it's direct.
B O.K., I'd like to make a reservation.

3 ▶ Listen to the rest of the conversation in exercise 2. Which flight does the passenger select?

From Taipei, Taiwan to Osaka, Japan			
Flight No.	Lv.	Arr.	Stops
891	800 a	1125 a	0
656	1000 a	315 p	1
911	400 p	725 p	0

4 ▶ Work with a partner. Play these roles.

Student A You want to fly from Chicago to Montreal. Call the airline and ask for information. (Student B is the airline agent.) First find out how long each flight takes. Then choose a flight and make a reservation. You may use these expressions.
I'd rather (not) . . .   *change planes*   *nonstop*

Student B You work at the reservations desk of Atlantic Airlines. A customer (Student A) calls about flights from Chicago to Montreal. Answer Student A's questions, using the timetable on page 111. Be sure to give information about all the flights. You may use these expressions.
It depends on . . .   *direct*   *takes longer*   *makes a stop*

78. Have we met somewhere before?

Terry Enders has just knocked at Doug Lee's door.

1

Terry Hi! My name's Terry Enders. I'm Kate's friend.

Doug Oh, hi, Terry. I'm Doug Lee. You live upstairs, right?

Terry That's right, in the apartment above yours. . . . Mmmm, something smells delicious. Are you cooking?

Doug Well, it depends on what you call cooking. I'm just making some chicken . . . very basic. Uh, would you like to come in?

Terry Thanks, no, I don't want to disturb you. I was just wondering if you knew Kate's new phone number. I can't seem to find it.

Doug Uh, no, I don't. But if you call the old number, there'll probably be a recording telling you the new one.

Terry Oh, you know, you're right. Why didn't I think of that?

Doug You know, it's funny. . . . Your name sounded really familiar when Kate first mentioned you, and now that I see you, you look familiar too. Have we met somewhere before?

Terry No, I don't think so. You're probably confusing me with my sister. She's pretty well known.

Doug Oh, really?

Terry Listen, I'd better run back upstairs. I'm expecting a phone call. I'll talk to you later, O.K.? Nice meeting you!

Doug Nice meeting you, too.

2. Figure it out

Say *True, False,* or *It doesn't say.*

1. Doug invites Terry to dinner.
2. Terry's sister is a well-known actress.
3. Doug suggests that Terry call Kate's old number to find out her new one.
4. Doug thinks that maybe he's seen Terry before.
5. Terry hears her phone ringing and runs back to answer it.

3. Listen in

Terry gets a phone call from her sister, Laura, who tells her that Chuck is in Los Angeles. Read the questions below. Then listen to the conversation and choose *a* or *b*.

1. Chuck is still in Los Angeles because
   a. he couldn't get a flight back.
   b. he decided to stay longer.

2. If Chuck isn't back in time for dinner,
   a. Laura won't go to Terry's.
   b. Laura will go to Terry's alone.

79. Your turn

Look at the pictures and discuss these questions in groups.

1. Which activity do you think is the most interesting? Why?
2. Do you do any of these things in your free time or on weekends? If so, which ones?
3. What are some other things that you like to do in your free time or on weekends?
4. Where would you rather spend your free time—indoors or outdoors? Why?

going to the beach

reading

camping

roller blading

playing tennis

How to say it

Practice the conversation.

A If it's nice, I'll go camping this weekend.

B It's supposed to be. If it isn't too hot, maybe I'll go to the beach.

80.

What do you like to do on the weekend?

Dan Orlofsky

I like to go to flea markets and garage sales. My parents have an antique shop, and I'm always looking out for bargains for them. For myself, I like to buy an old table or chair that someone else would just walk right past. Then, when the weather isn't so nice, I stay home and refinish it, turning it into a beautiful piece of furniture.

Maggie Hogan

I love to go biking! Two years ago I got an exercise bike to lose weight. After a few months, I got bored with being indoors, so I bought a used bike and started going for short rides to run errands. Now I plan day trips in my neighborhood. When you drive a car, you don't notice much. It's amazing how much more you notice when you're biking. I'd much rather go sightseeing by bike.

Richard Woo

Every weekend that it doesn't rain I play golf with a group of my friends. The four of us get up early and meet at the golf course before eight o'clock—otherwise, it gets too crowded. We carry our own bags and never use a cart. That way we get some extra exercise. When we're done, we go to the clubhouse for an early lunch.

Barbara Green

My favorite thing to do on the weekend is to go to the beach. The beach is beautiful all through the year. If the weather is cold, I put on some warm clothes and go for long walks on the shore with my dog. I also like to collect shells or just sit on the rocks and think. When the weather is hot, I enjoy swimming or just lying in the sun.

Bill Wilson

On the weekends I like to catch up on my reading—novels, magazines, newspapers, even the comic strips! If the weather is nice, I'll take a good book to the park and stay there reading for hours. Then I'll stop off at the bookstore on my way home and take a look around. In my opinion, there's nothing as relaxing as a good book.

Sara Turco

Weekends are for going hiking with my husband and kids. We live near some beautiful mountains with many different trails to choose from. Sometimes we combine hiking with fishing and then we camp out overnight. We really enjoy cooking dinner over a campfire and spending a night under the stars!

1. Answer the questions.

1. Which person likes to walk on the beach in cold weather?
2. Which person likes to go camping with his or her family?
3. Which person enjoys playing golf with friends?
4. Which person likes to go shopping for old furniture?
5. Which person enjoys reading in the park?
6. Which person likes to go sightseeing on a bicycle?

2. Match these words and phrases with their definitions.

1. flea market
2. antique shop
3. bargain
4. refinish
5. day trip
6. shell

a. hard covering of a clam, crab, or other sea animal
b. to paint or decorate woodwork again
c. store that sells valuable old objects such as paintings and furniture
d. journey to a place and back again on the same day
e. outdoor place where people sell used objects for very low prices
f. something that is sold at a price that is lower than usual

Review of units 8–11

1 ► Sam and his wife, Joan, get an early-morning phone call from Sam's brother, Fred. Complete Fred's part of the conversation.

Sam *(Yawn)* Hello?

Fred _____

Sam Uh, well, as a matter of fact, I was sleeping. *(Yawns)* Just let me try to open my left eye.

Fred _____

Sam Saturday night? No, I don't think we're busy.

Fred Aunt Thelma and Uncle Max are going to be in town. _____ _____

Sam Dinner? That sounds great, but I'll have to check with Joan. Believe it or not, she's still asleep.

Fred _____

Sam I hope we can too. Listen, I'll call you back after I talk to Joan, O.K.?

2 ► A few hours later, Joan asks Sam about the phone call. Combine each pair of sentences in brackets [ ] into one sentence.
► Listen to check your work.

Joan [What did Fred want? Tell me.] *Tell me what Fred wanted.*

Sam Aunt Thelma and Uncle Max are going to be in town on Saturday. Fred is having them over for dinner, and he wants us to come.

Joan [Which ones are Thelma and Max? I can never remember.]

Sam The ones with the big dogs.

Joan Oh, that's right. [How long are they going to be in town? Do you know?]

Sam Just one night.

Joan Is that all? . . . [What is Fred having for dinner? Do you know?]

Sam He's making his special chicken.

Joan Just as I thought. Well, we're not doing anything Saturday. [What time does he want us to be there? Be sure to find out.]

Sam O.K. I'll call him later and ask.

3 ▶ **Jim Williams is calling about a job that was advertised in the paper. Complete the conversation. Combine each pair of sentences in brackets [ ] into one sentence, and fill in the blanks to complete the questions.**

Ms. Ford Angela Ford speaking.

Jim Williams Hello, Ms. Ford. My name is Jim Williams. [I'm calling about the job. You advertised the job in Sunday's paper.] *I'm calling about the job that you advertised in Sunday's paper.*

Ms. Ford Oh, yes, the receptionist's job. [Well, we're looking for someone. The person should have some experience.] Have you worked as a receptionist before?

Jim Williams [Yes, I used to work for a company. The company sold computer equipment.] [I answered the phone and greeted people. The people came into the office.]

Ms. Ford Oh, well, that sounds good. Could you come in for an interview tomorrow at 2:00?

Jim Williams Yes, I'll be there. You're on Washington Street, _____ ?

Ms. Ford Yes, at 256 Washington Street. Do you know _____ ?

Jim Williams I think so. It's the tall building on the corner of Park and Washington, _____ ?

Ms. Ford That's right. By the way, [Do you have a letter of reference from the company? You used to work for the company.]

Jim Williams Yes, I do. I'll bring it with me tomorrow.

4 ▶ **Work in a group. These people have all applied for the job described in the ad. Read the ad and the qualifications of the three candidates below. Then compare the candidates and decide which person is best for the job.**

Linda Marino speaks Spanish better than David Rogers and Miyuki Mori, but Miyuki Mori . . .

RECEPTIONIST/ADMINISTRATIVE ASSISTANT to work in international sales office. Requires excellent word-processing and office skills. Should speak Spanish, get along well with people, and have a pleasant telephone voice. Previous sales office experience preferred, but not essential. Excellent salary and benefits. Call 555-7200 between 9 and 5 weekdays.

Miyuki Mori has ten years' experience as an administrative assistant in a sales office. She has excellent word-processing skills. She's pleasant and cheerful and enjoys working with people. She speaks a little Spanish, but not very well.

David Rogers has worked as an administrative assistant in a sales office for the past three years. He has good word-processing skills, and he speaks Spanish fairly well. He's quiet but very pleasant and easy to get along with.

Linda Marino has done part-time secretarial work for the past six months and is looking for a full-time job. Her word-processing skills are fair. She speaks Spanish fluently, but she hasn't done sales work before. She's very friendly and outgoing.

5 ▶ **Read the three ads. Then listen to the three conversations and match each conversation with the correct ad.**

a.
PHYSICAL THERAPIST
Opening for experienced physical therapist in modern physical therapy department of a hospital. Excellent benefits. 555-3426.

b.
SOCIAL WORKER
Excellent opportunity in private social services agency serving elderly clients. Master of Social Work preferred. 555-2419.

c.
STAFF ACCOUNTANT IN HOSPITAL
Opening for accountant with experience in the hospital or medical field. Degree preferred. Call 555-9203.

6A ▶ **Student A follows the directions below.**
▶ **Student B follows the directions on page 124.**

Student A Call about one of the ads in exercise 5. Ask questions that weren't answered in the ad. Find out the name of the hospital or agency that placed the ad, where it is located, and when the job begins. Begin some of your questions with *Could you please tell me . . . ?*

7 ▶ **Carol runs into her friend Amy and has this conversation. For each set of brackets [ ], combine the unfinished sentence with the question that follows it.**
▶ **Listen to check your work.**

Carol Barry and I are thinking of going to Thailand for our vacation this year.

Amy That sounds exciting! When are you planning to go?

Carol Sometime during the summer. [We're not quite sure . . . When are we going?] *We're not quite sure when we're going . . .* [It depends on . . . When can we both take a month off from work?]

Amy [Do you know . . . ? Who used to live in Thailand?] My brother.

Carol No kidding! [I'd love to ask him . . . Where should we go and what should we see?]

Amy Well, he's coming to visit sometime next month. Why don't we all get together then?

Carol I'd really like that. [Do you happen to know . . . ? What's the weather like in Thailand]?

Amy I think it's pretty hot and humid most of the year. And there's a rainy season. [But I'm not sure . . . When is it?] [I think it depends on . . . What part of the country are you going to?]

Carol [Well, let me know . . . When is your brother coming here?]

Amy I will, as soon as I find out.

6B
▶ Student B follows the directions below.
▶ Student A follows the directions on page 123.

Student B You work in the personnel office of one of the places mentioned in the ads below. Answer Student A's questions, using the information below.

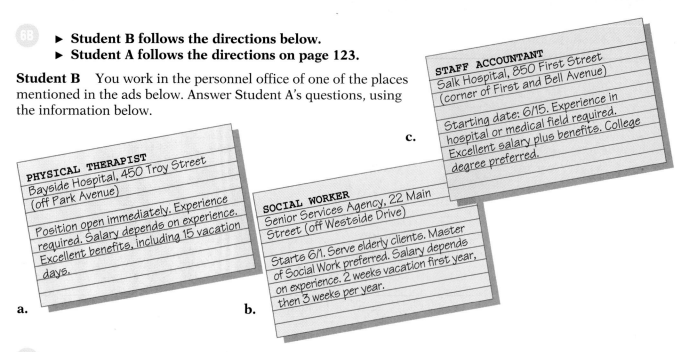

c.

STAFF ACCOUNTANT
Salk Hospital, 850 First Street
(corner of First and Bell Avenue)

Starting date: 6/15. Experience in hospital or medical field required. Excellent salary plus benefits. College degree preferred.

PHYSICAL THERAPIST
Bayside Hospital, 450 Troy Street
(off Park Avenue)

Position open immediately. Experience required. Salary depends on experience. Excellent benefits, including 15 vacation days.

a.

SOCIAL WORKER
Senior Services Agency, 22 Main Street (off Westside Drive)

Starts 6/1. Serve elderly clients. Master of Social Work preferred. Salary depends on experience. 2 weeks vacation first year, then 3 weeks per year.

b.

8 ▶ Barry and Carol want to make sure they haven't forgotten anything. Barry is looking at their "Things to do" list and asking Carol questions. Match the two parts of each sentence.

1. Our plane leaves at 8:05,
2. You have our passports,
3. You've called your parents to say good-bye,
4. Tom is picking us up at 6:00,
5. Tom knows what time the plane leaves,
6. Sue's going to water the plants,
7. Sue's picked up our key,
8. You're carrying the traveler's checks in your bag,

a. haven't you?
b. hasn't she?
c. aren't you?
d. isn't she?
e. doesn't it?
f. isn't he?
g. doesn't he?
h. don't you?

THINGS TO DO!
• *Call Carol's parents*
• *Arrange pick up with Tom*
• *Give Sue key and ask her to water plants*
• *Take traveler's checks and passports*
• *Depart 8:05*

9 ▶ Two people at a party are talking about Bob, Tony, Susan, and Jane. Use the phrases in the box to complete the conversation.
▶ Practice the conversation with a partner.

who's wearing the red dress
I used to work with
with the beard
who's talking to Bob

A I was just talking to Bob Miller.
B Oh, which one is he?
A He's the one _____ . He introduced me to his wife, Susan. She's the woman _____ .
B Who's the tall man _____ ?
A Don't you remember? That's Tony Lopez. He's a really nice guy.
B Oh, yeah. And who's the other woman?
A That's Jane Lin. She's someone _____ .

Tony   Bob   Jane   Susan

P R E V I E W

FUNCTIONS/THEMES	LANGUAGE	FORMS
State a conclusion	This must be a great place to eat!	*Must*
Decide what to order in a restaurant	Do you know what you're going to order? I can't make up my mind. I can't decide between the lobster and the steak. I'm going to get the cherry cheesecake.	
Ask for something	Could I have another cup of coffee, please? Could we have some more water, please?	*Another, some/any more, and something/anything else* with count and mass nouns
Talk about how food tastes Talk about how things smell, taste, sound, feel, look, seem	How's your lobster? It tastes kind of funny. Everything looks delicious. It smells awful.	Sense verbs
Identify a song or a person	It sounds familiar, but I don't remember what it's called. He looks familiar, but I'm not sure who he is.	
Ask for permission	Do you mind if I open the window? No, not at all. I'd rather you didn't.	

Preview the conversations.

pasta

steak

chef's salad

Work with a partner and discuss these questions.

1. Which of these dishes would you like to order in a restaurant?
2. What other foods do you like to have when you eat out?
3. Are there any special foods that you like to order in a restaurant that you don't usually eat at home?

lobster

cheeseburger

81. This must be a great place!

Four friends are trying a new restaurant.

The Silver Spoon

MENU

- 🍴 Charbroiled steak with parsley potatoes
- 🍴 Lobster in champagne-vinegar sauce
- 🍴 Chef's salad with our special house dressing
- 🍴 Pasta primavera
- 🍴 Cheeseburger—"the works"—on sesame bun with lettuce, tomato, and onion slices. Served with french fries.

A

Joe Look at that crowd! This must be a great place to eat!

Janet It's a good thing we made a reservation.

Meg I know just what I want—lobster in champagne-vinegar sauce.

Joe Mmm, that sounds good. You know, I think I might have that too.

Meg Do you know what you're getting, Mike?

Mike I can't make up my mind. I can't decide between the lobster and the steak.

Meg Oh, get the lobster. You can always get a steak.

Waiter Are you ready to order?

Janet Yes, I'll have the pasta primavera, please.

Waiter I'm sorry, there's no more pasta. We just ran out of it. . . .

Janet Oh, then I'll have the chef's salad.

B

Meg Everything looks delicious!

Mike Uh, this isn't mine. I ordered steak—well done.

Waiter Oh, I'm really sorry. I'll bring your steak right away.

Joe Do you mind if we start?

Mike Oh, no, please do.

Janet Oh, waiter, could I have another glass, please? This one has lipstick on it.

Waiter I'm so sorry. I'll get you another one.

Joe And could we have some more water, please?

Waiter Of course.

Mike Does anyone mind if I smoke?

Janet Well . . . actually, I'd rather you didn't.

Mike Oh, well, no problem. How's your lobster, Meg?

Meg Hmm, it tastes kind of funny. Maybe it's the sauce. Here, taste it.

Mike Uh, no thanks. Why don't you send it back and get something else?

Meg Good idea. I think I'll get a steak.

C

Mike Listen to that song! Do you know what it is?

Joe Hmm, it sounds familiar, but I don't remember what it's called.

Meg It's "Smoke Gets in Your Eyes."

Janet Speaking of smoke, I smell smoke—don't you?

Meg It must be a cigar. Ugh. It smells awful.

Joe No, I think it's coming from the kitchen. (*Starts coughing*)

Waiter (*To Mike*) Your steak, sir. (*To Meg*) Yours will be here in a few minutes, ma'am.

Mike Well, it *is* well done.

Figure it out

1. Listen to the conversations and choose the correct answers.

1. a. Meg, Mike, Joe, and Janet had to wait a long time to get a table.
   b. The restaurant is very crowded.

2. a. Janet doesn't want Mike to smoke.
   b. Mike smokes a cigar while he waits for his dish.

3. a. Meg ordered the steak because they were out of pasta.
   b. Janet wanted to order the pasta.

4. a. Mike took Meg's advice and ordered the lobster.
   b. Mike ordered the steak.

5. a. Mike's dish came later than the others.
   b. Everyone started eating at the same time.

6. a. Mike's steak is overcooked.
   b. Mike's steak is well done, just the way he likes it.

2. Match.

1. My glass isn't clean.
2. We're out of water.
3. Listen to that song.
4. I smell smoke.
5. Do you mind if I start?

a. I'll bring you some more.
b. No, please do.
c. It sounds familiar.
d. I'll bring you another one.
e. It must be a cigar.

82. Do you know what you're going to order?

STATE A CONCLUSION • *MUST*

1 ▶ Listen to the conversation and practice it with a partner.
▶ Practice similar conversations, using the pictures and the sentences below or your own ideas. Use *must* to state a conclusion.

A Look at that crowd! This must be a great place to eat!
B It's a good thing we made a reservation.

crowd   traffic   line   dark clouds

Some exclamations	Some conclusions	It's a good thing . . .
Look at that crowd!	There's an accident.	we already have tickets.
Look at all that traffic!	There's a storm coming.	we made a reservation.
Look at the line!	This is a great place to eat.	we're almost home.
Look at those dark clouds!	This is a really good play.	we're not driving that way.

DECIDE WHAT TO ORDER IN A RESTAURANT

2 ▶ Ellen and Tim are having lunch at The Sandwich Shop. Listen to the conversation. Check (√) the items that Ellen decides to order. Circle the items that Tim decides to order.

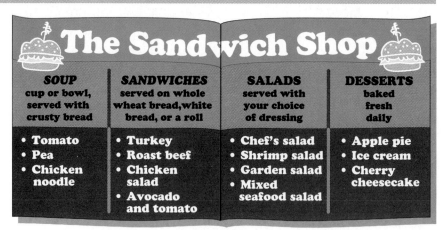

The Sandwich Shop

SOUP cup or bowl, served with crusty bread	SANDWICHES served on whole wheat bread, white bread, or a roll	SALADS served with your choice of dressing	DESSERTS baked fresh daily
• Tomato	• Turkey	• Chef's salad	• Apple pie
• Pea	• Roast beef	• Shrimp salad	• Ice cream
• Chicken noodle	• Chicken salad	• Garden salad	• Cherry cheesecake
	• Avocado and tomato	• Mixed seafood salad	

3 ▶ Listen to the three possible conversations and practice them with a partner.
▶ Act out similar conversations about what you are going to order in a restaurant, using the menu above or the menu on page 126.

A Do you know what you're going to order?

B I'm going to get the avocado and tomato sandwich. How about you?
A . . .

B Well, the shrimp salad sounds good. I think I might get that. How about you?
A . . .

B I can't make up my mind. I can't decide between the chef's salad and the garden salad. How about you?
A . . .

4 ▶ **Listen to the conversation and practice it with a partner.**

A Could I have another cup of coffee, please?
B I'll get it for you right away. Anything else you'd like?
A Yes. Could you bring some more cream, please?
B Sure.

5 ▶ **Study the frames:** *Another, some/any more, and something/anything else*

I'd like	another	roll.
	some more	rolls. coffee.
	something else.	

Count Nouns

another roll
some more rolls
another cup of coffee
another glass of water

I don't want	another	roll.
	any more	rolls. coffee.
	anything else.	

Mass Nouns

some more cheese
some more bread
some more coffee
some more water

another roll → another *one*
some more coffee → some more

6 ▶ **You've invited a friend over for dinner. Your friend's plate is empty, and there's a lot of food left on the table. Complete the conversation with** *another (one), some (any) more,* **or** *something (anything) else.* **There may be more than one answer.**
▶ **Listen to a possible conversation.**

A How about _____ piece of chicken, Sally?
B No, thanks. It was delicious, but I'm really full.
A Are you sure? There's still a little salad. Why don't you have _____ ?
B No, really, I can't eat _____ .
A Well, then, can I get you _____ to drink?
B Could I have _____ glass of water, please?
(During dessert)
A Mmm. These cookies are terrific!
B Well, here, have _____ .
A Oh, I really shouldn't eat _____ , but maybe I will have _____ .

7 ▶ **Work with a partner. You've already had a serving of the items below. Ask your partner for more. Then change roles.**
Could I have another cup of coffee?

bread

a cup of coffee

a glass of mineral water

cheese

strawberries

a piece of cheesecake

83. It tastes delicious.

▶ Listen to people tasting food. What will they say next? Write the numbers next to the matching pictures.

☐ This tastes awful. ☐ Delicious! ☐ This tastes kind of strange.

▶ Listen to the two possible conversations and practice them with a partner.
▶ Practice similar conversations about food in the pictures and menus in this unit.

A How's your lobster?

B Mmm. Delicious.   **B** Hmm. It tastes kind of funny.

A Why don't you send it back and get something else?

It tastes . . .

delicious.
pretty good.
kind of funny/strange.
spoiled.
awful.

TALK ABOUT HOW THINGS SMELL, TASTE, SOUND, FEEL, LOOK, SEEM • SENSE VERBS

▶ **Study the frames: Sense verbs**

Sense verbs with nouns		Sense verbs with adjectives		
Smell	this rose.	It	**smells**	wonderful.
Taste	this soup.	It	**tastes**	strange.
Listen to	this song.	It	**sounds**	familiar.
Feel	this sweater.	It	**feels**	soft.
Look at	John.	He	**looks**	terrific.
		He	**seems**	thinner.

▶ Complete the conversations with appropriate sense verbs. Make sure to put the verbs in the right tense.
▶ Listen to check your work.

1. **A** I ___smell___ onions.
   B It's this soup I'm making.
   A Mmm . . . It _____ great.
   B Here, _____ it.
   A Hmm, it _____ familiar.
   B That's because it's your mother's recipe.

2. **A** _____ Al. His face is all red.
   B You're right. He _____ awful. *(Al walks over.)*
   C I think I have a fever.
   B Let me _____ your forehead. You're burning up! *(Al coughs.)*
   A And _____ that cough. It _____ terrible. Go home!

3. **A** I haven't seen Freddy in so long. He sure has changed.
   B Yeah, he _____ much thinner.
   A Even his voice _____ different.
   B Oh? I wasn't really _____ him. I was talking to his wife. She _____ very nice.

IDENTIFY A SONG OR A PERSON

5 ▶ **Listen to the three possible conversations and practice them with a partner. Hum part of a song that you know.**

A Listen to this song. (*Hums.*) Do you know what it is?

B It's *"Smoke Gets in Your Eyes."*

B It sounds familiar, but I don't remember what it's called.

B I've never heard it before.

6 ▶ **Listen to the three possible conversations and practice them with a partner.**
▶ **Act out similar conversations, using the pictures below.**

A Do you know who this is?

B Michael Jackson.

B He looks familiar, but I'm not sure who he is.

B I've never seen him before.

The answers to this exercise are on page 165.

ASK FOR PERMISSION

7 ▶ **Listen to the two possible conversations and practice them with a partner. Ask for permission to do something, using the phrases in the box or your own ideas.**

A Do you mind if I open the window?

B No, not at all. Go right ahead.

B Well, I'd rather you didn't.

Do you mind if I...

sit here?
close the window?
turn on the heat?
turn off the radio?

84. I've been thinking . . .

Laura goes to the airport to meet Chuck, who has just come back from a job interview in Los Angeles.

1

Chuck You look happy. Are you glad to see me?

Laura *(Laughs)* Well, you look happy, too! You seem much more relaxed.

Chuck Yeah, I was pretty depressed for a while. It was nice to get away for a few days. But it's good to be back too.

Laura So, tell me about the interview. How did it go?

Chuck It went well. . . . As a matter of fact, it went very well. They offered me the job.

Laura Oh . . . well, that's terrific. You must feel really good about it. Are you . . . uh . . . thinking of accepting it?

Chuck I haven't told them yet. I have until Friday to let them know. I can't make up my mind. I love Chicago and, of course, you're here. You know how I feel about that. But this is the best opportunity I've ever had.

Laura It sounds as if you've already made up your mind.

Chuck Hey, don't look so sad. You know, I've been thinking a lot these last few days. This will probably sound crazy to you . . . I mean, I know you have your job, and your sister and your friends here, but I'd like you to go with me. . . . Listen, Laura, why don't we get married?

Laura Chuck . . . do you mind if I sit down for a minute?

2. Figure it out

Say *True, False,* or *It doesn't say.*

1. Chuck has been in Los Angeles for four days.
2. Chuck was depressed before his trip.
3. Chuck has already accepted the job offer.
4. Chuck wants Laura to marry him.
5. Laura wants to sit down because her feet hurt.

3. Listen in

The next day at work, Laura has something on her mind. Listen to the conversation. What two things did she forget?

85. Your turn

You are at the International Soup Café. Read about the soups on the menu. Then work in groups of three and play these roles.

Students A and B You are customers at the café. Discuss the different soups and decide which ones to order. If you have ever had any of these soups, make a recommendation. Then give the waiter or waitress your order.

Student C You are the waiter or waitress. Take the orders of Students A and B.

The International Soup Café adds a new soup to its menu every month. What soup do you think it should add this month? Recommend a soup that's popular in your country, and describe it to your classmates.

The International Soup Café

"WE HAVE SOUPS FROM ALL OVER THE WORLD."

Beid bi lamoun
A Middle Eastern chicken soup made with eggs, lemon, and rice. Served with buttered toast.

Won Ton Soup
A soup from China. Dumplings stuffed with pork served in a delicious broth.

Minestrone Soup
An Italian soup made with garden-fresh vegetables and beans. Topped with Parmesan cheese. Served with Italian bread.

Vichyssoise
A wonderful hot-weather soup from France. Made with leeks, potatoes, chicken broth, and cream. Served cold with French bread.

Gazpacho
A cold Spanish soup made from tomatoes, onions, cucumber, green peppers, garlic, vinegar, olive oil, and bread. The name is Arabic for "soaked bread."

Chicken Gumbo Soup
From New Orleans. A soup made from chicken, tomatoes, onions, peppers, okra, and other fresh vegetables. Served with black bread.

All of our soups come with salad, coffee, and dessert.

How to say it

Practice the phrases. Then practice the conversation.

could you   [kúdʒə]
would you   [wúdʒə]
why don't you [wáɪdontʃu]

A Could you pass the salt? This soup tastes really bland.
B Would you like to taste my gazpacho? It's delicious.
A Oh, it *is* good.
B Why don't you order some?
A I think I will. I'm sorry I didn't order gazpacho before.

86.

Restaurant Guide

★ • ★ • ★ • ★ • ★ • ★ • ★ • ★ • ★ • ★ • ★ • ★ • ★ • ★

Look at the names of the five restaurants in the guide. What kind of food do you think each one specializes in?

Richard's Steak House ★★★★/E

This superb steak house has been a landmark for over fifty years. The attention to detail assures you that the setting and service are as perfect as your meal, whether it's a quiet dinner for two, a business lunch, or a small party. From the prime rib to the filet mignon, all the meat dishes are cooked exactly the way you want. Richard's also has an excellent wine selection to complement your meal.

Treasures of the Sea ★★★★/E

Located right on the waterfront, this busy seafood restaurant is a very popular spot. It's best to make reservations if you plan on dining while watching the sun set over the bay. Try the shrimp in garlic sauce, a big favorite, or the delicious lobster for two—and be sure to wear your bibs! If you just want a taste of lobster without all the fuss, order the lobster bisque soup. Whether you come through the front door, or sail right up to the dock, you'll enjoy this wonderful restaurant, where the fish and other seafood are fresh and truly a treasure.

Garden Delight ★★★/M

This attractive, new dining spot is great for people who are interested in healthy eating. The chef uses only the freshest ingredients and makes sure the dishes are high in taste and low in fat. There are many salads to

choose from, as well as homemade soups and steamed vegetables over brown rice. And you'll love the freshly baked whole grain rolls served with your meal. Try to get a table in the outdoor garden, or come by on a weekend for brunch and classical music.

California Pizza Plus ★★★/I–M

At California Pizza Plus you can satisfy your tastebuds by designing your own pizza pie. You can select the standard pizza toppings such as mushrooms, cheese, or peppers, or (for more adventurous diners), you can go tropical with pineapple, banana, or coconut pizza! Whether you like your pizza plain or loaded with exotic toppings, this is the place for fun and mouth-watering food. The restaurant is decorated with old movie posters and the staff is efficient and friendly.

On the Run ★/I

If you're in a hurry, you should be able to get a good, quick meal—but not here. The service is slow and the food is not very appetizing. It seems like the microwave has replaced the chef. French fries are greasy, and the salad may have been fresh once, but not when it gets to your table.

Rating System ★ Poor ★★ Fair ★★★ Very Good ★★★★ Excellent

Prices **E** = expensive **M** = moderate **I** = inexpensive

1. **Which restaurant would you go to . . .**

   a. with a vegetarian?
   b. with someone who likes beef?
   c. for a casual, relaxed, but inexpensive evening?
   d. to celebrate a very special occasion?

2. **Which restaurant do you think you would prefer?**
3. **Write a short review of a restaurant you know.**

P R E V I E W

FUNCTIONS/THEMES	LANGUAGE	FORMS
State a conclusion	You must be getting a cold.	*Must*
Figure out where you left something Talk about possibilities	They may be in your coat pocket. I might play tennis.	*May* and *might*
Talk about quantity	There's only a little left. There's not much left. We must not have any more then.	Count and mass nouns
Make a request	Is there anything you need? Could you pick up a roll of paper towels?	
Ask where something is Talk about location	Could you tell me where the carrots are? They're behind the lettuce. It's on the top shelf, next to the spaghetti. They're in the refrigerator, on the bottom shelf.	Prepositions
Apologize for being late	I'm sorry I'm late. I got caught in traffic. I just got here myself.	

Preview the conversations.

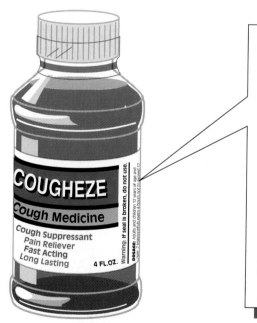

DOSAGE
Adults and children 12 years of age and over: 2 teaspoonfuls every 4 hours, not to exceed 12 teaspoonfuls in a 24-hour period.
Children 6 to under 12 years: 1 teaspoonful every 4 hours, not to exceed 6 teaspoonfuls in a 24-hour period.
Children 2 to under 6 years: 1/2 teaspoonful every 4 hours, not to exceed 3 teaspoonfuls in a 24-hour period.
Children under 2 years: Consult your physician.
Do not exceed recommended dosage.

Read the label on the cough medicine bottle. Then find another way to say these expressions.

1. doctor
2. no more than
3. every 24 hours
4. older than 11
5. amount to take
6. ask the advice of

87. There are only a few left.

Anna and her husband, Victor, have just gotten home from work. Anna isn't feeling well

A

Victor Hi! Sorry I'm late. I got caught in traffic.

Anna I just got home myself.

Victor Hey, you don't look very good.

Anna I must be getting a cold. I've had this terrible headache since I got up, and I've been snee . . . A-A-ATCHOO! . . . sneezing all day.

Victor Bless you.

Anna Thank you.

Victor Look, why don't you go upstairs and lie down? I'll bring you some aspirin.

B

Victor I don't see any aspirin in the medicine cabinet.

Anna We must not have any more.

Victor Oh, wait, here's the bottle, behind the cough medicine. Hmmm, there's only one left. I'll go to the drugstore and get some more. Is there anything else we need?

Anna Could you get some more ti . . . ATCHOO! . . . tissues? There are only a few left in the box. ATCHOO!

Victor Bless you.

Anna Thank you. Oh, and could you get some more tea? We just ran out of tea bags.

Victor Any special kind?

Anna No, I don't care.

Victor Now what did I do with my car keys?

Anna Take mine. They're in my bag.

Victor Where's your bag?

Anna It must be downstairs. Look on the kitchen table. If it's not there, it might be on the coffee table in the living room.

C

Victor Could you tell me where the tissues are, please?

Pharmacist All the way in the back, against the wall. (*A few minutes later*) Have you found them? They're way up on the top.

Victor Oh, yes, I see them.

D

Victor Do you have tonight's paper?

Pharmacist We may not have any more. If there are any left, they're up in front with the magazines.

Victor I've already looked there.

Pharmacist Well, then we must be out of them.

Figure it out

1. Listen to the conversations and choose the correct answers.

1. a. Victor walked home from work.
   b. Victor drove home from work.

2. a. Anna got home just before Victor did.
   b. Anna has been home all day.

3. a. Anna felt fine when she got up.
   b. Anna has had a headache all day.

4. a. There are no tea bags left.
   b. Anna just bought some tea bags.

5. a. Victor left his car keys downstairs.
   b. Victor doesn't know where his car keys are.

6. a. The drugstore doesn't sell newspapers.
   b. The drugstore doesn't have any newspapers left.

2. Find another way to say it.

1. I just got home too.
2. I'm almost sure I'm getting a cold.
3. Do we need anything else?
4. Maybe we're out of them.
5. I'm almost sure we're out of tea bags.

3. Complete each sentence with *tea*, *tea bag*, or *tea bags*. Some items have more than one answer.

1. We only have a few _____ left.
2. Do we have any more _____ ?
3. There's just a little _____ left.
4. We don't have many _____ left.
5. We have a lot of _____ left.
6. There's only one _____ left.

88. You must be getting a cold.

STATE A CONCLUSION • *MUST*

▶ **Complete each conversation with a conclusion from the box. Use *must*.**
▶ **Listen to check your work.**
▶ **Practice the conversations with a partner.**

Some conclusions

You're getting a cold.
You're starving.
You have a cavity.
You're exhausted.

1. **A** I've been sneezing all day.
   B *You must be getting a cold* .

2. **A** I have a terrible toothache.
   B _____ .

3. **A** I haven't sat down all day.
   B _____ .

4. **A** I haven't eaten all day.
   B _____ .

FIGURE OUT WHERE YOU LEFT SOMETHING • *MAY* AND *MIGHT*

▶ **Listen to the conversation. Check (√) the things the man is looking for.**

___ keys   ___ glasses   ___ briefcase   ___ appointment book

▶ **Listen to the conversation and practice it with a partner.**
▶ **Act out similar conversations, using the pictures in exercise 2 and the places in the box.**

A Now, what did I do with my glasses?
B They may be in your coat pocket.
A No, I just looked there.
B Well, they might be on your desk.
A Good idea. I'll check there.

Some places to look

in your coat pocket	on your desk
in your car	on the table
in your briefcase	in your bedroom
at work	at home

4 ▶ **Molly and David are talking about their plans for the weekend. Listen to the conversation. Check (√) the things that Molly says she might do this weekend.**

___ go to the beach   ___ play golf   ___ visit some friends   ___ stay home and read

5 ▶ **Listen to the two possible conversations and practice them with a partner.**
▶ **Act out similar conversations with the sentences in the box or your own ideas.**

A What are you doing this weekend?
B If the weather is good, I might play tennis.
What about you?

A I'm not sure.
I may just stay home.

A I might not do anything.

What are you doing this weekend?

I might/may play tennis.
I might/may just stay home.
I might/may go dancing.
I might/may see a movie.
I might/may not do anything.

6 ▶ **Study the frames: May, might, and must**

Affirmative statements

She	**may** **might**	have	a headache.
		stay	home tomorrow.
		be getting	sick.

| He | **must** | have | the flu. |
| | | be working | too hard. |

Negative statements

He	**may** **might**	**not**	have	any aspirin.
			come	to work tomorrow.
			be eating	the right food.

| She | **must** | **not** | have | a car. |
| | | | be getting | enough sleep. |

Use *may* and *might* to express possibility.

She *may/might* have a headache. (It's possible that she has a headache.)
I *may/might* not go to work tomorrow. (It's possible that I won't go to work tomorrow.)

Use *must* to state a logical conclusion.

He *must* have the flu. (I'm almost sure that he has the flu.)
He *must* not be getting enough sleep. (I'm almost sure that he isn't getting enough sleep.)

Like *can* and *should*, the modal auxiliaries *may*, *might*, and *must* have the same form for all pronouns and are followed by the base form of the verb. Compare the formation of sentences in the present and present continuous tenses.
She *has* a headache. → She *may have* a headache.
He's *getting* the flu. → He *might be getting* the flu.
He *has* a cold. → He *must have* a cold.

7 ▶ **Complete the conversations, using *may*, *might*, or *must* in your answers.**

1. **A** I wonder where Ali is.
   B *He might be at work*_____ . I'll call his office.

2. **A** Is Julia Fox there?
   B Julia Fox? _____ the wrong number.
   A Oh, I'm sorry.

3. **A** I'll see you at the theater.
   B _____ . It depends on how much work I have.

4. **A** I haven't eaten all day.
   B _____ .
   A No. Actually, I'm not hungry at all. I have a terrible headache.
   B _____ .

5. **A** I've been exhausted all week.
   B _____ .
   A That's very possible. I never get to sleep before midnight.

89. Do we have any cough medicine?

1 ▶ **Study the frames: Count and mass nouns**

Count nouns	Mass nouns
Do we have any tea bags?	Do we have any cough medicine?
There are only a few left.	There's only a little left.
There aren't many left.	There's not much left.
There's only one left.	

There's only a little left.   There are only a few left.

2 ▶ **Listen to the two possible conversations and practice them with a partner.**
▶ **Act out similar conversations about the things in the pictures below.**

A Do we have any cough medicine?
B We may be out of it. Look in the medicine cabinet.

A Oh, here it is. I found it. There's only a little left.

A I've already looked there.
B We must not have any more, then.

Some places to look
in the medicine cabinet
under/over the (kitchen) sink
in the bathroom closet
in the desk drawer

shampoo

paper clips

envelopes

tea bags

detergent

toilet paper

3 ▶ **Complete the note with *a few, a little, much,* or *many.***

Linda,

I wanted to do the laundry, but there's only _____ detergent. There's not _____ soap left either, so I've gone to the supermarket. I'll pick up some eggs and napkins too. There are only _____ eggs left in the refrigerator and not _____ napkins.
I'll see you when I get back.

4 ▶ **Listen to the conversation. Check (√) the things that the man and woman need.**

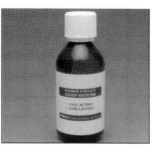

___ cough medicine

___ tissues

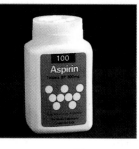

___ aspirin

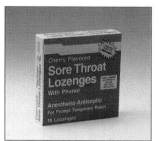

___ throat lozenges

5 ▶ **Complete each conversation with one of the responses in the box.**
▶ **Listen to check your work.**
▶ **Practice the conversations with a partner.**

> We just ran out of them.
> We just ran out of it.
> I just used the last one.
> I just ate the last one.

1. **A** Do you have any newspapers left?
   B No, I'm sorry.

_____

2. **A** Are there any sandwiches left?
   B No, there aren't.

_____

3. **A** Is there any more milk?
   B No, there isn't.

_____

4. **A** Do we have any more paper clips?
   B No, we don't.

_____

6 ▶ **Listen to the three possible conversations and practice them with a partner.**
▶ **Act out similar conversations. First request the items in the pictures below. Then ask for things you really need.**

A I'm going to the grocery store. Is there anything you need?

B Could you pick up a roll of paper towels? I just ran out of them.

> Other ways to say it
>
> Could you please get me . . . ?

A Sure. Any particular kind?

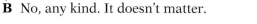

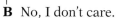

B Yes. Round-up.   **B** No, any kind. It doesn't matter.   **B** No, I don't care.

a roll of paper towels

a bottle of shampoo

some apples

a tube of toothpaste

a box of detergent

90. Could you tell me where the carrots are?

TALK ABOUT LOCATION • ASK WHERE SOMETHING IS • PREPOSITIONS

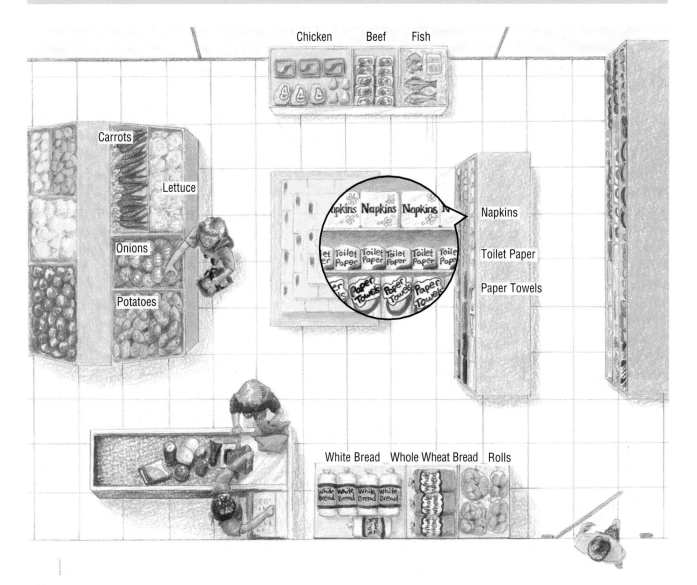

1. ► **Look at the floor plan of the supermarket and match the items with their location.**

1. The carrots are
2. The chicken is
3. The paper towels are
4. The bread is
5. The napkins are

a. (down) on the bottom, below the toilet paper.
b. in the front of the store, next to the cashier.
c. behind the lettuce.
d. in the back of the store, against the wall.
e. (up) on the top, above the toilet paper.

2. ► **Listen to the conversation.**
► **Work with a partner. Act out similar conversations about the items in the grocery store in exercise 1.**
► **Talk about the location of things in your classroom.**

A Could you tell me where the carrots are?
B They're behind the lettuce.
A And do you know where the ice cream is?
B Sorry, but I don't know.

Other locations
next to
across from
in front/back of
on the right/left

3 ► Linda is making spaghetti sauce. She's asking her roommate questions about where things are. Listen to the conversation and practice it with a partner.

Linda Do we have any olive oil?
Sally Yes. It's in the cabinet, on the top shelf, next to the spaghetti.
Linda And I need some fresh tomatoes.
Sally They're in the refrigerator, on the bottom shelf.

Cabinet

Olive Oil   Spaghetti

Tomato Paste   Green Beans

Refrigerator

Salt   Pepper

Sugar

Sink

Milk

Orange Juice

4 ► Work with a partner. Play these roles.

Student A You want to make some spaghetti sauce. Ask Student B about the location of the ingredients on the list.

Student B Answer Student A's questions, using the picture of the kitchen in exercise 3.

SPAGHETTI SAUCE
Ingredients:
• onions
• carrots
• tomatoes
• tomato paste
• olive oil
• salt
• pepper

Tomatoes   Carrots   Onions

APOLOGIZE FOR BEING LATE

5 ► Listen to the three possible conversations and practice them with a partner.
► Act out similar conversations, using the reasons in the box or your own ideas.

Some reasons for being late

I got caught in traffic.
I couldn't find a parking space.
My car wouldn't start.
I missed the bus/train.
I overslept.

A I'm sorry I'm late.
I got caught in traffic.

B Oh, that's O.K.
I had time to look at the menu before you came.

B Oh, that's O.K.
I just got here myself.

B Oh, that's O.K.
I've only been here for a little while.

91. I'm afraid we don't have many left.

Doug is shopping for a clock radio.

1

Clerk	Is there anything I can help you with, or are you just looking?
Doug	I'm looking for a clock radio. Are these the only ones you have?
Clerk	Yes, I'm afraid we don't have many left. . . . They were just on sale. Did you have a particular one in mind?
Doug	No, not really. I was just trying to get an idea of what there was.
Clerk	This one is very nice. It has an AM/FM radio, a lighted dial . . .
Doug	Does it come in another color?
Clerk	It did come in white, but I don't see any, so we must have sold the last one. The red one's quite attractive, though. Is it a gift or for yourself?
Doug	It's for myself. What about that one way up on top?
Clerk	That one's a little more expensive. Would you like me to get it down for you?
Doug	Please. . . . Do you mind if I try it?
Clerk	No, not at all. *(Doug turns on the radio.)*
Voice	Good afternoon and welcome to "A Little Afternoon Music." I'm your host, Laura Enders. We've got lots of wonderful . . .
Doug	Laura Enders!
Clerk	I beg your pardon?
Doug	Uh . . . nothing. I guess I'll take it.
Clerk	If you could step over here, please. . . .

2. Figure it out

Say *True, False,* or *It doesn't say.*

1. Doug is buying the radio as a gift.
2. The store doesn't have many clock radios left.
3. Doug buys the more expensive radio.
4. Laura Enders has her own radio show.
5. Doug needs a clock radio because he often oversleeps.

3. Listen in

Doug is listening to the weather report on his new radio. Read the statements below. Then listen to the report and choose *a* or *b*.

1. Sunday's temperature is going to be
   a. 5° (degrees) Fahrenheit.
   b. -15° (degrees) Fahrenheit.

2. It's going to be
   a. sunny.
   b. cloudy.

92. Your turn

Work in a group. Ellen didn't go to work today. Why not? Study the pictures and tell about Ellen's day yesterday.

1.
2.
3.
4.

Work with a partner. Act out the conversation in each picture.

How to say it

Practice the phrases. Then practice the conversation.

cár keys	hóuse keys	páper clips
cóat pocket	tóilet paper	tóothpaste

A Where are your car keys?
B They're in my coat pocket—with my house keys. O.K., let's go. What do we need from the store?
A Let's see. . . . We need toilet paper, paper clips, and toothpaste. Anything else?
B No, that's it.

Medical Advice

Before you read the article, read these statements and decide if they are *True* or *False*. Then read the article to see if you were right.

1. Vitamins can cure a cold.
2. You can catch a cold by touching something that a person with a cold has touched.

By Dr. Elaine Ramsey

DEAR DR. RAMSEY:

I seem to get colds all the time. Is there anything I can do to prevent them? What should I do after I've caught one?
—SNIFFLES

DEAR SNIFFLES:

The common cold is the most frequent of all illnesses. At any given moment, about one out of every eight people has a cold. Most people get colds by touching things that another person with a cold has used or touched. You can even catch a cold by shaking hands. So if someone you know has a cold, you should try not to use the same cups, glasses, dishes, or telephone. If you have to touch a person with a cold or handle something that the person has used, wash your hands immediately afterwards. Soap does not kill cold viruses, but running water can carry them away.

Although there is no cure for the common cold, doctors believe that vitamins can help prevent them. Many doctors recommend vitamin C to prevent colds, and some doctors suggest that you take large amounts when you begin to get cold symptoms. Yet it is not really known whether vitamin C is truly helpful.

The body needs healthy food to fight a cold. If you have a cold, you should eat well, but not overeat, and you should drink lots of liquids, especially fruit juices. Also be sure to get enough rest and stay warm. If your body aches, you can take one to two aspirin every four hours. Some research shows, however, that taking aspirin might make your cold last longer.

When you have a cold, you should also try to protect other people. Cover your mouth and nose with a tissue when you cough or sneeze. Put all your used tissues in a paper bag, and throw away the bag yourself so that no one else will have to touch it. Wash all objects that you touch with very hot water before anyone else uses them.

Use the information in the article to answer these questions.

1. How many people have colds right now?
2. How do most people catch colds?
3. What advice do doctors give about vitamin C?
4. What are three things you should do when you have a cold?
5. How can you protect other people when you have a cold?

PREVIEW

FUNCTIONS/THEMES	LANGUAGE	FORMS
Greet someone after a long time	I haven't seen you in so long! How have you been? You haven't changed a bit! I didn't recognize you at first. You've really changed!	Review: The present perfect
Talk about people you knew	Do you still keep in touch with anyone from school? I still get together with Rosa from time to time.	
Catch up on what someone has done	Have you seen any good movies recently? No, not in a long time. Neither have I.	Short negative responses
Ask about duration	How long have you been living in Toronto? I've been living here since last fall.	The present perfect continuous
Make a suggestion Accept or reject a suggestion	Why don't we go get coffee somewhere? Good idea. Let's go to the coffee shop on the corner. I'd like to, but I've got to get going.	

Preview the conversations.

Nancy's college graduation

Ten years later

Look at the pictures. Then discuss these questions with a partner.

1. How has Nancy changed since her graduation?
2. What were you doing five years ago? Ten years ago? What have you done since then? What are you doing now?
3. Has your life changed much in the last five (or ten) years? How?
4. Have you changed much in the last five (or ten) years? In what ways?

94. Catching up

Nancy Dodd and Dennis Miller, two old college friends from Harvard University, run into each other in Guadalajara, Mexico.

A

Nancy Dennis Miller?

Dennis Nancy Dodd? In Guadalajara? I don't believe it! Hey, you haven't changed a bit!

Nancy Neither have you!

Dennis Oh, come on now. I used to have more hair, didn't I?

Nancy Well, now that you mention it . . .

Dennis So, how have you been? What brings you to Guadalajara?

Nancy I'm here on vacation. You too?

Dennis Do I *still* look like a tourist? I live here.

Nancy You're kidding! How long have you been living here?

Dennis For three years.

Nancy Really? What do you do here?

Dennis Well, I'm studying Spanish, and I've been teaching English since last fall. How about you?

Nancy I'm an architect.

Dennis Hey, not bad.

Nancy And you're not going to believe this— I'm still living in Cambridge.

Dennis No kidding!

Nancy My husband's on the faculty at Harvard.

Dennis How long have you been married?

Nancy For five years.

Dennis Is your husband here?

Nancy Yes, he's back at the hotel, resting.

B

Dennis Gee, I haven't been back to Cambridge in years, not since we graduated . . . . Has it changed much?

Nancy Oh, not that much. You'd still recognize it! You know, it's great seeing you again. I've really lost touch with everyone from back then.

Dennis So have I. Let's keep in touch . . . .

Nancy Listen, why don't we go get some coffee somewhere?

Dennis Oh, I'd like to, but I've got to get going. I teach at four. But how about dinner? You and your husband can meet me after my class.

Nancy Sounds great!

Dennis Have you been to the Guadalajara Grill? It's very famous.

Nancy Not yet.

Dennis Well, I haven't been there in ages, so why don't we go there?

Nancy I'd love to.

Dennis Do you want to meet there at eight o'clock?

Nancy Sure. See you then.

Figure it out

1. Listen to the conversations and choose the correct answers.

1. a. Nancy and Dennis haven't seen each other recently.
   b. Nancy and Dennis have kept in touch since college.

2. a. Dennis has lost some hair since the last time he saw Nancy.
   b. Dennis thinks Nancy has changed a lot.

3. a. Nancy's husband is a student at Harvard.
   b. Nancy's husband teaches at Harvard.

4. a. Nancy's husband must be tired.
   b. Nancy's husband didn't come to Guadalajara.

5. a. Dennis still writes to some people he knew at Harvard.
   b. Dennis hasn't heard from any of the people that he and Nancy knew.

6. a. Dennis wants to have dinner before his class.
   b. Dennis wants to have dinner after his class.

2. Complete each sentence with *No, Not,* or *Neither*.

1. _____ have I.
2. _____ yet.
3. _____ kidding!
4. _____ since we graduated.

3. Find another way to say it.

1. Why are you in Guadalajara?
2. How long have you lived here?
3. from those days
4. I have to go.
5. for a long time

95. You haven't changed a bit!

1 ▶ These people all graduated from the same college ten years ago. Some have changed more than others. How have they changed? Match.

1. Jim
2. Robert
3. Andrea
4. Linda

a. let her hair grow.
b. used to have more hair.
c. wears glasses now.
d. has lost a lot of weight.
e. wears contact lenses now.
f. has a mustache now.

Jim Silver

Robert Barnes

Andrea London

Linda Campos

2 ▶ Linda hasn't seen Robert since they graduated from college. Listen to the conversation and practice it with a partner.
▶ Imagine you and your partner run into each other ten years from now. Use your imagination and act out a similar conversation.

Linda Robert Barnes?
Robert Linda Campos! I haven't seen you in so long! How have you been?
Linda Fine. How about you?
Robert Not bad. You know, I didn't recognize you at first. You've really changed!
Linda Well, I've lost a lot of weight. But, hey, you haven't changed a bit!
Robert Oh, come on. I used to have more hair.
Linda Well, now that you mention it . . .

TALK ABOUT PEOPLE YOU KNEW

3 ▶ Linda and Robert continue talking. Listen to the conversation and practice it with the same partner.

Linda Do you still keep in touch with anyone from school?
Robert Yes, I still get together with Rosa from time to time.
Linda And what about Andrea? Do you hear from her?
Robert Well, we used to write occasionally, but I haven't heard from her in over a year. What about you? Do you still keep in touch with anyone?
Linda No, I've really lost touch with everyone.

▶ Now continue the conversation you started in exercise 2 with your partner. Talk about people you both know.

Some ways to keep in touch

get together (with someone)
write (to someone)
hear from someone
call someone up
talk (to someone)
see someone

In present perfect negative statements, either *in* or *for* is used before a period of time.

in over a year, *for* over a year

4 ▸ **Jean and Bill run into each other at a party. Listen to the conversation and check (√) the things that Jean has done since she last saw Bill.**

__ gotten married
__ let her hair grow
__ moved back to California
__ lived in Chicago

5 ▸ **Listen to the two possible conversations and practice them with a partner.**
▸ **Act out similar conversations, using the questions and answers in the boxes and your own information.**

A Have you seen any good movies recently?

B Yes, I've seen a couple of good ones.

B No, not in a long time.

A Neither have I.

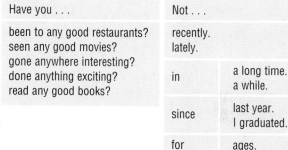

Have you . . .	Not . . .	
been to any good restaurants? seen any good movies? gone anywhere interesting? done anything exciting? read any good books?	recently. lately.	
	in	a long time. a while.
	since	last year. I graduated.
	for	ages.

6 ▸ **Study the frames: Short negative responses**

	Negative responses	Short negative responses
Do you ever go back to Cambridge?	I don't go back there very often.	**Not very often.**
Have you taken a vacation recently?	I haven't taken one since last summer.	**Not since last summer.**
Are you still teaching French?	I'm not teaching anymore.	**Not anymore.**
Have you been to the Guadalajara Grill?	I haven't been there yet.	**Not yet.**

7 ▸ **Complete each conversation with an appropriate short negative response. Use the phrases in exercises 5 and 6. There may be more than one answer.**

1. **A** Have you finished the homework?
   B _____ . I have a little more to do.

2. **A** Do you ever see Mary?
   B _____ . Maybe once or twice a year.

3. **A** You're still in college, aren't you?
   B _____ . I graduated in June.

4. **A** Have you seen any good movies recently?
   B No, _____ . It's been at least six months.

8 ▸ **Talk to your classmates. Ask questions about what they have and haven't done recently. Your classmates will use short negative responses whenever appropriate.**

96. How long have you been living in Toronto?

1 ▶ Listen to the conversation.
▶ Practice the conversation with a partner. Use your own information.

A How long have you been living in Toronto?
B I've been living here since last fall.
A How long have you been studying English?
B For a couple of years.
A Oh, you speak it really well.

2 ▶ Study the frames: The present perfect continuous

Information questions

How long	have	you they	been	working	here?
	has	he she		teaching	

Affirmative statements

I We They	've		been	working	here	for nine years.
He She	's			teaching		since 1993.

When the verbs *live*, *work*, *study*, and *teach* are used with expressions of duration, there is little difference in meaning between the present perfect and the present perfect continuous.

3 ▶ Listen to Frank Lynch and Martha Corning talk about themselves.
▶ Work with a partner and play these roles.

Student A Ask questions about Frank using *How long . . .?* and the present perfect continuous of *live* and *work*. Then answer Student B's questions about Martha and her husband.

Student B Answer Student A's questions about Frank. Then ask questions about Martha and her husband using *How long . . .?* and the present perfect continuous of *live, work, study,* and *teach.*

A *How long has Frank Lynch been working at Ace Plumbing?*
B *He's been working there . . .*

B *How long have Martha and John Corning been living in Washington, D.C.?*
A *They've been living there . . .*

Frank Lynch
Miami

Martha and John Corning
Washington, D.C.

4 ▶ **Listen to the three possible conversations and practice them with a partner.**

A Why don't we go get coffee somewhere?

B Good idea. Let's go to the coffee shop on the corner.

B I'd like to, but I've got to get going. I've got to get to the bank before it closes. But let's keep in touch. Here's my phone number . . .

B I'd like to, but I've got to get going. I'm supposed to be somewhere in five minutes. But let's get together another time. Are you doing anything on Saturday?

A I don't think I am.

B Well, I'm thinking of going to see the Picasso exhibit at the Art Institute. Why don't you join me?

A Sure. I'd love to.

Some suggestions

Why don't we . . .
    go get coffee somewhere?
    go get something to eat?
    take a walk?
    go see a movie?

5 ▶ **Work in groups of three. Play these roles.**

Student A Make a suggestion to do something after class.

Student B Accept Student A's suggestion and suggest a place.

Student C Reject Student A's suggestion, give a reason, and make a suggestion for getting together at another time.

Some reasons for refusing

I've got a class in a little while.

I've got to get back to work.

I've got to get to the bank before it closes.

I'm supposed to be at the dentist in ten minutes.

I'm supposed to pick up my sister at the airport.

97. Here we are again.

Laura and Terry are flying home to Seattle for the holidays.

1. Listen in

Laura has just arrived at the airport, where Terry is waiting for her. Read the statements below. Then listen to the conversation and say *True* or *False*.

1. Terry has been waiting for Laura for a long time.
2. Laura hasn't eaten, but Terry has.
3. Laura isn't going to buy something to eat at the snack bar.

2

Laura	I got a letter from Chuck today.
Terry	Oh, what did he have to say?
Laura	Well, all in all, he seems pretty happy. He likes Los Angeles, and he's meeting some really nice people.
Terry	Does he still want you to go there?
Laura	He says he does.
Terry	And how are you feeling?
Laura	Sad. I miss him. But I think I've made the right decision, at least for now.
Terry	(*Noticing Doug*) I don't believe it! Here comes the guy who lives downstairs from me.
Doug	If it isn't the Enders sisters! Well, here we are again, Laura!
Terry	Hey, wait a minute. . . . Do you two know each other?
Laura	You *do* look awfully familiar. Have we met somewhere?
Doug	On my first flight from Seattle to Chicago. Doug Lee . . . I was coming here for a job interview. You were reading a Stephen King novel. . . .
Laura	Oh right! You've got a good memory.
Doug	So, how did you like it?
Laura	What?
Doug	The Stephen King novel.
Laura	Great ending!
Doug	Yeah, I thought so, too. Oh, and you'll be happy to hear, I got the job.
Laura	Congratulations! What kind of job is it? . . .

3. Figure it out

Say *True, False,* or *It doesn't say.*

1. Chuck moved to Los Angeles.
2. Laura has decided to stay in Chicago.
3. Laura doesn't think about Chuck anymore.
4. Laura doesn't recognize Doug at first.
5. Terry and Doug planned to take the same plane.
6. Doug hasn't seen his family since he moved to Chicago.

98. Your turn

Read the letter from Terry Enders to Kate Simmons. Then work in a group and talk about what has happened to Terry, Laura, Doug, and Chuck in the past five years.

Dear Kate,

I'm sorry I haven't written for so long, but I've been really busy! So much has happened since you moved to Denver. I can't believe it's been five years since I last saw you! The big news is that I got married six months ago. I married Bill Lambert. You must remember him. He used to work at the Community Services Agency. Doug Lee introduced us! Doug is still working at the agency. In fact, he's running the whole place. When Mr. Dow left, Doug got the job as director of the agency.

My sister Laura is still here in Chicago, too, but she's not working at the radio station anymore. She's on television now! She's the executive producer and host of a new talk show called "Chicago Edition." She's been working there for a year. The show is a big success, but Laura hasn't changed a bit. I'm really happy that her career is going so well.

Do you remember Laura's old boyfriend, Chuck? The one who moved to Los Angeles? Laura doesn't see him anymore of course, but they still write each other from time to time. Well, Laura tells me that he's not only married now, but he's the father of twin girls! He met someone a couple of years ago and got married.

What's going on in your life? After five years, you must have a lot of news, too. Do you have any plans to come back and visit Chicago? You know you're welcome to stay with us. It would be great to see you and catch up!

Please write soon!

Terry

P.S. Laura sends her best.

Write a letter to a friend you haven't seen in a long time. Tell him or her how your life has changed.

How to say it

Practice the words. Then practice the conversations.

gotten [gátn]   written [rítn]   eaten [ítn]

1. **A** I haven't gotten a letter from Mark in six months.
   B Neither have I, and I've written to him twice. I hope he's O.K.

2. **A** Have you eaten at Frank's Steak House recently?
   B No. I haven't eaten there since last summer.

99. What does your handwriting say about you?

Do you think that a person's handwriting can tell you anything about their personality? Look at exercise 1 and see if you can guess the answers. Then read the article to find out.

People have been fascinated by handwriting for a long time. The first book on graphology, the study of handwriting, was written in 1632, and since that time hundreds of books have been published on the subject.

Graphologists believe that you can learn a lot about people's personalities by looking at the way they write. Some of the characteristics they look at are slant—whether your letters point forward or backward, pressure—whether you press hard or only lightly on the paper, and the size of capital letters. As shown below, each of these characteristics can reveal different personality tendencies. For example, if you slant your letters forward, you are probably an outgoing, friendly person.

SLANT

forward — an outgoing, friendly person

up and down — a logical person

backward — a person with many secrets

PRESSURE

heavy — a very emotional person

light — an impractical person

CAPITAL LETTERS

Fancy — a vain person

Large — a confident person

small — a shy person

Typical — an unimaginative person

Graphologists also look at which parts of the letters seem larger or more important. For this purpose they have divided the letters into three zones or areas.

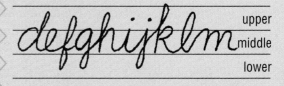

According to one graphologist, if the part of the letter in the upper zone is very large compared to the part in the middle zone, then the writer is probably idealistic. If the part in the lower zone is very large, it shows that the writer is very interested in money and success. If the letters of all the zones are well balanced, the writer is probably practical.

Whether or not you close letters such as *a* or *o* also says something about your personality.

open — If the letters *a* or *o* are open, the writer is probably an honest person who likes to talk.

closed — If these letters are closed, the writer is good at keeping a secret.

Police have asked graphologists to help them solve crimes, and businesses have used handwriting samples to choose employees. So the next time you sit down to write a letter, fill out a form, or even write your name—be careful. You may be telling people more than you think.

---

1. **Read the magazine article. Then say *True* or *False*.**

1. The way you write can tell a graphologist about your personality.
2. People have studied handwriting for more than 350 years.
3. Emotional people press very hard when they write.
4. When someone's handwriting has a backward slant, he or she probably also leaves letters open at the top.
5. Most shy people make big capital letters.

2. **Look at Terry's letter on page 155. What does Terry's handwriting say about her personality according to the article?**

3. **Can you analyze your own handwriting? What can you say about your own personality from your handwriting?**

Review of units 12-14

1 ▶ Larry and his wife, Beth, are at Larry's twentieth high school reunion. Norm, an old high school friend, greets Larry. Listen to the conversation.

Norm Larry! How have you been?

Larry Norm! It's good to see you again. You know, it's been twenty years, but you haven't changed a bit.

Norm Well, you don't look much different either. I hear you spent some time in South America.

Larry Yes, Beth and I lived in Buenos Aires for ten years. By the way, this is my wife, Beth. Beth, this is Norm Lewis.

Norm Nice to meet you, Beth.

Beth Nice to meet you, too.

Norm So, are you living in the States now?

Beth Yes, we moved to San Francisco two years ago, when we came back from Argentina.

Norm That really sounds great, living in South America. I haven't been there, but I visited Mexico six years ago—my wife and I went there for our honeymoon. That's the last time I was out of the country.

Larry Oh, so you're married?

Norm Yes, and I have two kids too. Tell me, do you ever get back to Argentina?

Beth Unfortunately, we haven't managed to make a trip since we've been back.

▶ Complete each of these statements with a time expression beginning with *for*, *in*, or *since*. Use the information in the conversation.

1. Larry hasn't seen Norm _____ .
2. Larry and Beth have lived in San Francisco
   _____ .
3. Larry and Beth haven't been back to Buenos Aires _____ .
4. Norm has been married _____ .
5. Norm hasn't been out of the U.S. _____ .

2 ▶ Imagine you and your classmates are at a school reunion. Greet someone you haven't seen since graduation. Catch up on what that person has done since graduation and keep the conversation going. Use the phrases below or your own ideas.

How have you been?　　　*Do you ever . . . ?*　　　*What have you been doing since . . . ?*
Do you still . . . ?　　　*Have you . . . ?*　　　*How long have you been . . . ?*

3 ▶ **Norm and Larry are talking about Chris Walker, an old classmate. Listen to their conversation and put a check (√) next to Chris in the picture. (Chris can be a man's name or a woman's name.)**

4 ▶ **Here are some other conversations taking place at the reunion. Complete each conversation with the correct form of one of the phrases in the box. Use the prepositions in parentheses where necessary. There may be more than one answer.**

get together (with)	lose touch (with)
hear from	keep in touch (with)
move back (to)	live (in)

1. **A** Do you ever see Liz Rogers?
   B We used to write, but I haven't _____ her in a long time.

2. **A** It's so great seeing you again.
   B Yes, we really ought to _____ more often.

3. **A** How long have you been _____ San Francisco?
   B For almost two years.

4. **A** Do you still _____ the people you knew in Buenos Aires?
   B No, I've really _____ everyone there.

5. **A** When did you _____ Montreal?
   B Six months ago.

6. **A** Have you _____ Alicia Marcos?
   B Not for a long time.

5 ▶ **Larry and Beth are flying back to San Francisco after the reunion. When they get to the airport, Larry can't find the tickets. Complete Beth's part of the conversation, using the words in parentheses.**

Larry Now what did I do with the tickets?
Beth _____ (may)
Larry I just looked there.
Beth _____ (might)
Larry I've already looked there, too. I hope I didn't leave them in the hotel room.
Beth Now I remember! They were on the bed, and I picked them up. _____ (must)

6 ► Larry and Beth are back at their apartment in San Francisco. Listen to their conversation and check (√) the things they need to buy.

SHOPPING LIST

o milk
o eggs
o butter
o cheese
o coffee
o tea
o sugar
o bread
o crackers
o fruit
o vegetables
o meat

7 ► **Work with a partner. Play these roles.**

Student A You are at the supermarket and want to buy the things on the shopping list in exercise 6. Ask Student B about the location of the things on the list.

Student B You work at the supermarket. Answer Student A's questions, using the picture of the supermarket below and the prepositions in the box.

in the front	next to
in the back	across from
on the top	in front/back of
on the bottom	on the right/left
against	

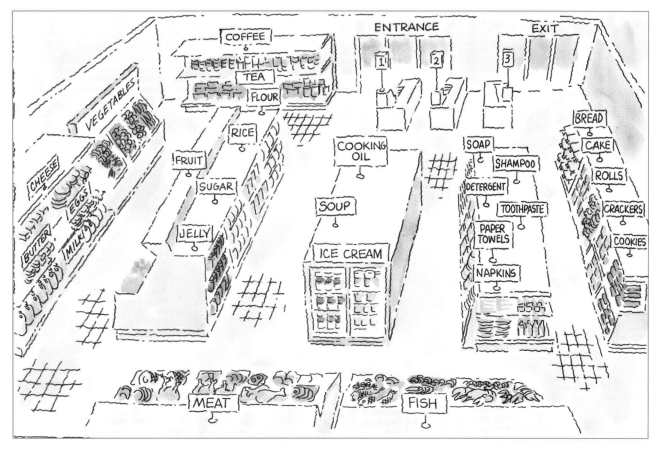

8 ▶ **Beth and Larry are having guests over for dinner. Everyone has something nice to say about the meal. Complete the conversation. Use the correct form of these verbs: *taste, smell, sound,* or *look*. There may be more than one answer.**

Kate Oh, your table _____ so nice.
Frank And something _____ wonderful.
Bill It must be the chicken.
Beth You're right. We make it with peppers and lots of garlic.
Sue It _____ delicious.
Larry Well, help yourselves before it gets cold.
Beth *(A few minutes later)* So, how does it _____ ?
Kate Wonderful.
Frank You're right. It really _____ great.

9 ▶ **Work with a partner. Play these roles.**

Student A Student B is a dinner guest in your home. You're serving chicken, string beans, french fries, and salad. Student B's plate is almost empty and there's food left on the table. Offer Student B some more food. Use the expressions in the box below.

| a lot (left) | some more | still some (left) | another |
| a little (left) | something else | a few (left) | |

Student B You are a dinner guest in Student A's home. Compliment the food and respond to Student A. You may use the expressions in the box below.

| a little | some | a few |
| some more | another | |

10 ▶ **Listen to the first part of each conversation and choose the best response.**

1. a. I'm sorry. We just ran out of it.
   b. I'm sorry. We just sold the last one.

2. a. Oh, that's O.K. I just got here myself.
   b. Oh, that's O.K. Go right ahead.

3. a. Yes. Could you bring me the check?
   b. No, I haven't made up my mind yet.

4. a. Could you pick up some aspirin?
   b. Any kind. It doesn't matter.

5. a. It's on the bottom shelf.
   b. They're next to the tomatoes.

6. a. She looks familiar, but I'm not sure who she is.
   b. I've never seen it before.

7. a. It might be in your coat pocket.
   b. It may be in your car.

8. a. Not anymore.
   b. Not yet.

9. a. No, I don't mind.
   b. No, this seat is taken.

10. a. So have I.
    b. Neither have I.

VOCABULARY LIST

This list includes both productive and receptive words introduced in Student Book 3. Productive words are those which students use actively in interaction exercises. Receptive words are those which appear only in opening conversations, comprehension dialogues, readings, and instructions, and which students need only understand. The following abbreviations are used to identify words: V = verb, N = noun, ADJ = adjective, R = receptive. Page numbers indicate the first appearance of a word.

SUPPLEMENTARY VOCABULARY

IRREGULAR VERBS

Base form	Simple past	Past participle	Base form	Simple past	Past participle	Base form	Simple past	Past participle
be	was, were	been	get	got	gotten	see	saw	seen
beat	beat	beaten	give	gave	given	sell	sold	sold
become	became	become	go	went	gone	send	sent	sent
begin	began	begun	grow	grew	grown	set	set	set
bend	bent	bent	have	had	had	shake	shook	shaken
bite	bit	bitten	hear	heard	heard	shoot	shot	shot
blow	blew	blown	hide	hid	hidden	shut	shut	shut
break	broke	broken	hit	hit	hit	sing	sang	sung
bring	brought	brought	hold	held	held	sit	sat	sat
build	built	built	hurt	hurt	hurt	sleep	slept	slept
buy	bought	bought	keep	kept	kept	slide	slid	slid
catch	caught	caught	know	knew	known	speak	spoke	spoken
choose	chose	chosen	lay	laid	laid	spend	spent	spent
come	came	come	lead	led	led	stand	stood	stood
cost	cost	cost	leave	left	left	steal	stole	stolen
cut	cut	cut	lend	lent	lent	stick	stuck	stuck
deal	dealt	dealt	let	let	let	strike	struck	struck
dig	dug	dug	lie	lay	lain	sweep	swept	swept
do	did	done	lose	lost	lost	swim	swam	swum
draw	drew	drawn	make	made	made	swing	swung	swung
drink	drank	drunk	mean	meant	meant	take	took	taken
drive	drove	driven	meet	met	met	teach	taught	taught
eat	ate	eaten	pay	paid	paid	tear	tore	torn
fall	fell	fallen	put	put	put	tell	told	told
feed	fed	fed	quit	quit	quit	think	thought	thought
feel	felt	felt	read	read [rèd]	read [rèd]	throw	threw	thrown
fight	fought	fought	ride	rode	ridden	understand	understood	understood
find	found	found	ring	rang	rung	wear	wore	worn
fit	fit	fit	rise	rose	risen	win	won	won
fly	flew	flown	run	ran	run	write	wrote	written
forget	forgot	forgotten	say	said	said			

ANSWERS

Preview the conversations, page 101

apt	apartment	mod	modern
avail	available	N	north
bldg	building	nr	near
BR	bedroom	rm	room
eves	evening	st	street
immed	immediately	sub	suburban
lge	large	transp	transportation
loc	location	utils	utilities

Exercise 7, page 131

(from left to right) Michael Jackson, James Dean, Tina Turner, Boris Karloff as Frankenstein

ACKNOWLEDGMENTS

ILLUSTRATIONS

Storyline illustrations by Anna Veltfort: pages 2, 3, 10, 16, 17, 20, 30, 40, 54, 64, 74; 28 (bottom right), 76 (bottom),78 (middle right), 88, 98, 108, 118, 132, 144, and 154; pages 34, 39 (top), 70 (top), 72 (top), 78 (bottom), 79, 80 (bottom), 84 (top), 92, 93, 107, 116, 117, 130, 138, (top) 145, 152, 157, 158, 159 (top), and 160 by Anne Burgess; pages 14, 15, 43, 44, 45, 46 (top right), 73 (bottom right), 126 and 127 by Hugh Harrison; pages 9, 16, 17,18, 66 (bottom), 68, 69, 128, and 129 by Randy Jones ; pages 7, 26, 27, 36, 37, 39 (bottom right), 46 (middle left and right), 50, 57, 58, 59, 62, 70, 71 (bottom right), 72 (bottom), 73, 86, 94, 96, 104, 106, and 114 by Gene Myers; pages 121, 131, 136, 137, and 140 by Charles Peale; pages 141 (middle), 142, and 143 (top) by Janet Pietrobono; pages 4, 5, 8, 61, 63 by Chris Reed; pages 103, 106, 124, 151, 153 (bottom), and 159 (bottom) by Bot Roda; pages 1, 19, 48, 51, 53, 60, 71 (top left, middle, and right), 77, 78 (top right), 84 (bottom), 85, 97, 138 (bottom), and 141 (bottom) by Arnie Ten; pages 112, 113, 122, and 153 (top) by Rod Thomas; page 76 by Jan Watkins. Handwriting, page 75, by Terry TenBarge.

PHOTOS

Page 5 (top left) by Shinichi Kanno/FPG International; pages 5 (top middle), 6 (top right), and 95 (top) by Will & Deni McIntyre/Photo Researchers; page 5 (top right) by Art Stein/Photo Researchers; page 6 (first left) by L. Grant/FPG International; pages 6 (second left), 6 (fourth left), and 6 (fourth right) by Travelpix/FPG International; page 6 (second right), 56 (top right), 65 (top middle), 89 (top left) by Comstock; page 6 (third left) by Bill Bachman/Photo Researchers; page 6 (third right) by Dale E. Boyer/Photo Researchers; page 11 (top right) by Haroldo and Flavia de Faria Castro/FPG International; page 11 (top left) by Stan Osolinski/FPG International; page 11 (middle right) by Mark Anderson/Camera Press London/Globe Photos; page 11 (bottom left) by Thomas Craig/FPG International; page 11 (bottom right), 28 (top middle), 38 (bottom), 119 (top and middle right), 120 (fifth and sixth), 122 (left), 124, 125 (top and bottom right), 129 (top left), and 140 (bottom left) by Superstock; page 12 (top left) by Rob Lang/FPG International; page 12 (bottom right) by Doug Plummer/Photo Researchers; page 13 (bottom left) by Rob Goldman/ FPG International; page 13 (bottom middle) by John T. Turner/FPG International; pages 13 (bottom right), and 22 (second) by Michael Krasowitz/FPG International; page 18 (first left) by Four by Five; page 18 (first right) by FPG International; page 18 (bottom left) by Chester Higgins, Jr./Photo Researchers; page 18 (bottom right) by M.B. Duda/ Photo Researchers; page 21 (top) and (middle) by Richard Hutchings/Photo Researchers; page 21 (bottom) by Ed Hoy/FPG International; page 22 (first) by Jeff Kaufman/FPG International; page 22 (third) by United Nations; page 22 (fourth) by Dick Luria/FPG International; page 23 (bottom left) by Adam Scull/Globe Photos; pages 23 (bottom right), 24 (top right), 25 (top right), 63 (bottom left), (bottom middle), (bottom right), 81, 82, 83, 87, 89 (top and bottom right), 102, 103, 140 (top left and right, bottom middle and right), 141 (first, second, and fourth), 147 (right), 150 (second, fourth, sixth, eigth, and ninth) by Frank Labua; page 28 (top left) by Ch. Petit/Agence Vandystadt/ Photo Researchers; pages 28 (top right) and 29 (top left) by Paolo Koch/Photo Researchers; page 28 (bottom left) by Adam Hart-Davis/Science Photo Library/ Photo Researchers; page 28 (bottom middle), 96 (bottom right) and page 100 (middle) by Dave Bartruff/FPG International; page 28 (bottom right) by Hiroshi Harada/Dunq/Photo Researchers; page 29 (top right) by Victor Englebert/Photo Researchers; page 29 (bottom right) by Suzanne Murphy/FPG International; pages 31 (top right), (middle left), (middle right), (bottom left) by Photofest; pages 33 and 41 courtesy of Joan Karis; page 35 (top) from the collection of L. Milton Warshawsky/Culver Pictures; page 48 (top right and bottom right), and 49 (top left) by Roberto Lessia; page 55 (bottom right) by Steve Vidler/ Leo de Wys; page 56 (bottom right) by Tim Holt/Photo Researchers; page 63 (top left) by Daniel Quat/FPG International; page 63 (top right) by Raul Rubiera/FPG International; page 63 (bottom left), 65 (top right) by Tom Tracy/The Stock Shop; page 63 (bottom right) by Gary Buss/FPG International; page 65 (top left) by David Frazier/Photo Researchers; page 65 (bottom left) by Eunice Harris/Photo Researchers; page 65 (bottom middle) by Margaret Miller/Photo Researchers; page 65 (bottom right) by Ray Malace/FPG International; page 67 (top right) by Lok, Inc./FPG International; page 67 by Frederick McKinney/FPG International; page 73 (top right) by Porterfield-Chickering/Photo Researchers; page 73 (bottom right) by Charles Mayer/Photo Researchers; page 80 (top left) by Ron Chapple/FPG International; page 80 (middle left) by Culver Pictures; page 80 (middle right) by Jose Luis Banus/FPG International; page 89 (top left) Comstock; page 89 (bottom left) by Reginald Wickham; page 90 by Paul Markow/FPG International; page 91 by Dick Dietrich/FPG International; page 95 (bottom) by Ulrike Welsch/Photo Researchers; page 96 (top left) by Ken Reid/FPG International; page 96 (top middle) by Lee Snyder/Photo Researchers; page 96 (top right) by Gary Buss/FPG International; page 96 (bottom left) by Elizabeth Simpson/FPG International; page 96 (bottom middle) by Bonnie Sue Rauch/Photo Researchers; pages 99 (first), 122 (right), and 148/149 (background) Four By Five; page 99 (second) by John Moss/Photo Researchers; page 99 (third) The Telegraph Colour Library/FPG International; page 99 (fourth) by Mathias Oppersdorff/Photo Researchers; page 100 (top) by William Katz/Photo Researchers; page 100 (bottom) by Museo Pio-Clementino, Vaticano/Art Resource; page 109 (top left) by Alan McGee/FPG International; page 109 (top middle) by J. Messerschmidt/FPG International; page 109 (top right) by Wes Thompson/Stock Market; page 109 (bottom left) by Charles Krebs/Stock Market; pages 110 (top); page 110 (bottom left) by O'Brien & Mayor Phot'y /FPG International; page 110 (bottom right) by Abarno /Stock Market; page 119 (middle left) by Gabe Palmer/Stock Market; page 119 (bottom left) by Paul Barton/Stock Market; page 119 (bottom right) by Michael P. Gadonski/Photo Reseachers; page 120 (first) by Glenn McLaughlin/Stock Market; page 120 (second) by Roy Morsch/Stock Market; page 120 (third) by Dick Luria/FPG International; page 120 (fourth) by Michael Keller/Stock Market; page 122 (middle) by Rob Goldman/FPG International; pages 125 (top left) and 129 (top middle) by Molkenthin Studio/Stock Market; page 125 (top middle) by Gerald Zanetti/Stock Market; page 125 (bottom left) by Ulfert Beckert/The Image Bank; page 129 (top right) by Nini Mascardi/The Image Bank; page 129 (bottom left) by Michael Skott/The Image Bank; page 129 (bottom middle) by Giampiccolo Images/FPG International; page 129 (bottom right) by Steven Mark Needham/Envision; page 131 (first) by James Smeal/Ron Galella, Ltd.; page 131 (second and fourth) by Photofest; page 131 (third) by Ron Galella, Ltd.; page 150 photos courtesy of David Riccardi, Stephanie Karras, Freddy Flake, and Paula Williams; page 140 (top middle) by Gerard Fritz/FPG International; page 141 (third) by Science Photo Library/Photo Researchers; page 147 (left) courtesy of Nancy Leonhardt; pages 148 and 149 (foreground) by Frank Labua and Molly Pike Riccardi; and page 152 (left) by Richard Hutchings/Photo Researchers.

REALIA

Pages 6, 12, 13, 16, 19, 21, 22, 23, 26, 27, 28, 29, 31, 32, 33, 37, 38, 41, 42, 47, 48, 50, 52, 53, 55, 56, 60, 66, 67, 75, 76, 77, 80, 81, 85, 86, 90, 91, 94, 95, 99, 100, 101, 104, 105, 106, 107, 110, 111, 120, 124, 126, 128, 133, 134, 135, 146, and 156 by Siren Design.

ꟶRMISSIONS

'What You're Worth Before You Seek a Raise," (p. 66). Reprinted by permission of Cynthia Hanson. First appeared in *Chicago* ꟼOMANEWS.